Across the Empty Quarter

The Arabian Desert, 1947

WILFRED THESIGER

Across the Empty Quarter

GREAT
JOURNEYS

PENGUIN BOOKS

Published by the Penguin Group
Penguin Books Ltd, 80 Strand, London WC2R ORL, England
Penguin Group (USA) Inc., 375 Hudson Street, New York, New York 10014, USA
Penguin Group (Canada), 90 Eglinton Avenue East, Suite 700, Toronto, Ontario, Canada M4P 2Y3
(a division of Pearson Penguin Canada Inc.)
Penguin Ireland, 25 St Stephen's Green, Dublin 2, Ireland (a division of Penguin Books Ltd)
Penguin Group (Australia), 250 Camberwell Road, Camberwell, Victoria 3124, Australia
(a division of Pearson Australia Group Pty Ltd)
Penguin Books India Pvt Ltd, 11 Community Centre, Panchsheel Park, New Delhi – 110 017, India
Penguin Group (NZ), 67 Apollo Drive, Mairangi Bay, Auckland 1310, New Zealand
(a division of Pearson New Zealand Ltd)
Penguin Books (South Africa) (Pty) Ltd, 24 Sturdee Avenue, Rosebank, Johannesburg 2196, South Africa

Penguin Books Ltd, Registered Offices: 80 Strand, London WC2R ORL, England

www.penguin.com

Arabian Sands first published in Great Britain 1959
This extract published in Penguin Books 2007
1

Copyright © Wilfred Thesiger, 1959
All rights reserved

Inside-cover maps by Jeff Edwards

Typeset by Rowland Phototypesetting Ltd, Bury St Edmunds, Suffolk
Printed in England by Clays Ltd, St Ives plc

ISBN: 978-0-141-02549-0

Contents

Wilfred Thesiger (1910–2003) was born at Addis Ababa, Abyssinia (now Ethiopia). Educated at Eton and Oxford, he worked in the Sudan Political Service and later, for a year, as a Political Officer for the Ethiopian Emperor, Haile Selassie. During World War II Thesiger served with the Sudan Defence Force, SOE and SAS. In Arabia before the war Thesiger mapped areas of the Empty Quarter, the fabled southern desert, which he crossed twice, in 1946–7 and 1947–8. He attributed his survival in the face of often desperate thirst, near-starvation and tribal conflict largely to his Bedouin companions, whose inspiring courage and resilience offered challenges he was determined to meet.

Thesiger began his first crossing of the Empty Quarter from Salala, accompanied by a party of Bedouin including Salim Tamtaim, Musallim bin Tafl, Mabkhaut, Salim bin Kabina and Muhammad al Auf. On his second crossing Thesiger's companions included Salim bin Kabina, Salim bin Ghabaisha and Amair, of the Rashid.

When Thesiger left Arabia in 1950, the desert Arab culture for which he felt such admiration and affinity was already threatened by economic forces beyond his and his companions' control. Although he returned at intervals to the Emirates and Oman, Thesiger would never again experience the harsh yet rewarding life he had shared with his Bedouin tribesmen during his five 'most memorable' years in the Arabian deserts.

Preface: Why the Desert

I first realized the hold the desert had upon me when travelling in the Hajaz mountains in the summer of 1946. A few months earlier I had been down on the edge of the Empty Quarter. For a while I had lived with the Bedu a hard and merciless life, during which I was always hungry and usually thirsty. My companions had been accustomed to this life since birth, but I had been racked by the weariness of long marches through wind-whipped dunes, or across plains where monotony was emphasized by the mirages shimmering through the heat. There was always the fear of raiding parties to keep us alert and tense, even when we were dazed by lack of sleep. Always our rifles were in our hands and our eyes searching the horizon. Hunger, thirst, heat, and cold: I had tasted them in full during those six months, and had endured the strain of living among an alien people who made no allowance for weakness. Often, in weariness of body and spirit, I had longed to get away.

Now, in the Assir, I was standing on a mountainside forested with wild olives and junipers. A stream tumbled down the slope; its water, ice-cold at 9,000 feet, was in welcome contrast with the scanty, bitter water of the sands. There were wild flowers: jasmine and honeysuckle, wild roses, pinks and primulas. There were terraced fields of wheat and barley, vines, and plots of vegetables. Far below me a yellow haze hid the desert to the east. Yet it was there that my fancies ranged, planning new journeys while I wondered at this strange compulsion which drove me back to a life that was barely possible. It would, I felt, have been understandable if I had been working in some London office, dreaming of freedom and adventure; but here, surely, I had all that I could possibly desire on much easier terms. But I knew instinctively that it was the very hardness of life in the desert which drew me back there – it was the same pull which takes men back to the polar ice, to high mountains, and to the sea.

To return to the Empty Quarter would be to answer a challenge, and to remain there for long would be to test myself to the limit. Much of it was unexplored. It was one of the very few places left where I could satisfy an urge to go where others had not been. The circumstances of my life had so trained me that I was qualified to travel there. The Empty Quarter offered me the chance to win distinction as a traveller; but I believed that it could give me more than this, that in those empty wastes I could find the peace that comes with solitude, and, among the Bedu, comradeship in a hostile world. Many who venture into dangerous places have found this comradeship among members of their own race; a few find it more easily among people from other lands, the very differences which separate them binding them ever more closely. I found it among the Bedu. Without it these journeys would have been a meaningless penance.

[. . .]

The First Crossing of the
Empty Quarter

Wishing our hosts the safe keeping of God, we turned away across the Sands. As he walked along, al Auf held out his hands, palms upwards, and recited verses from the Koran. The sand was still very cold beneath our feet. Usually, when they are in the Sands during the winter or summer, Arabs wear socks knitted from coarse black hair. None of us owned these socks and our heels were already cracking from the cold. Later these cracks became deeper and very painful. We walked for a couple of hours, and then rode till nearly sunset; encouraging our camels to snatch mouthfuls from any plants they passed. They would hasten towards each one with their lower lips flapping wildly.

At first the dunes were brick-red in colour, separate mountains of sand, rising above ash-white gypsum flats ringed with vivid green salt-bushes; those we passed in the afternoon were even higher – 500 to 550 feet in height and honey-coloured. There was little vegetation here.

Musallim rode the black bull and led his own camel, which carried the two largest water-skins. Going down a steep slope the female hesitated. The head-rope attached to the back of Musallim's saddle tightened and slowly pulled her over on to her side. I was some way behind and could see what was going to happen

3

but there was no time to do anything. I shouted frantic-ally at Musallim but he could not halt his mount on the slope. I prayed that the rope would break, and as I watched the camel collapse on top of the water-skins I thought, 'Now we will never get across the Sands'. Al Auf was already on the ground slashing at the taut rope with his dagger. As I jumped from my saddle I wondered if we should have even enough water left to get back to Ghanim. The fallen camel kicked out, and as the rope parted heaved herself to her knees. The water-skins which had fallen from her back still seemed to be full. Hardly daring to hope I bent over them, as al Auf said 'Praise be to God. They are all right,' and the others reiterated 'The praise be to God, the praise be to God!' We reloaded them on to the bull, which, bred in the sands, was accustomed to these slithering descents.

Later we came on some grazing and stopped for the night. We chose a hollow sheltered from the wind, unloaded the water-skins and saddle-bags, hobbled the camels, loosened the saddles on their backs and drove them off to graze.

At sunset al Auf doled out a pint of water mixed with milk to each person, our first drink of the day. As always, I had watched the sun getting lower, thinking. 'Only one more hour till I can drink', while I tried to find a little saliva to moisten a mouth that felt like leather. Now I took my share of water without the milk and made it into tea, adding crushed cinnamon, cardamom, ginger, and cloves to the brew to disguise the taste.

Firewood could always be found, for there was no place in the Sands where rain had not fallen in the past, even if it was twenty or thirty years before. We could always uncover the long trailing roots of some dead shrub. These Arabs will not burn tribulus if they can find any other fuel, for *zahra*, 'the flower' as they call it, is venerated as the best of all food for their camels and has almost the sanctity of the date palm. I remember how I once threw a date-stone into the fire and old Tamtaim leant forward and picked it out.

Bin Kabina brewed coffee. He had stripped off his shirt and head-cloth, and I said, 'You couldn't take your shirt off if I had not rescued your loin-cloth for you.' He grinned, and said, 'What could I do? He asked for it,' and went over to help Musallim scoop flour out of a goatskin: four level mugfuls measured in a pint mug. This, about three pounds of flour, was our ration for the day and I reflected that there must be very few calories or vitamins in our diet. Yet no scratch festered or turned septic during the years I lived in the desert. Nor did I ever take precautions before drinking what water we found. Indeed, I have drunk unboiled water from wells, ditches, and drains all over the Middle East for twenty-five years without ill-effect. Given a chance, the human body – mine at any rate – seems to create its own resistance to infection.

When Musallim had made bread, he called to al Auf and Mabkhaut, who were herding the camels. It was getting dark. Though a faint memory of the vanished day still lingered in the west, the stars were showing, and the moon cast shadows on the colourless sand. We

5

sat in a circle round a small dish, muttered 'In the name of God', and in turn dipped fragments of bread into the melted butter. When we had fed, bin Kabina took the small brass coffee-pot from the fire and served us with coffee, a few drops each. Then we crouched round the fire and talked.

I was happy in the company of these men who had chosen to come with me. I felt affection for them personally, and sympathy with their way of life. But though the easy equality of our relationship satisfied me, I did not delude myself that I could be one of them. They were Bedu and I was not; they were Muslims and I was a Christian. Nevertheless, I was their companion and an inviolable bond united us, as sacred as the bond between host and guest, transcending tribal and family loyalties. Because I was their companion on the road, they would fight in my defence even against their brothers and they would expect me to do the same.

But I knew that for me the hardest test would be to live with them in harmony and not to let my impatience master me; neither to withdraw into myself, nor to become critical of standards and ways of life different from my own. I knew from experience that the conditions under which we lived would slowly wear me down, mentally if not physically, and that I should be often provoked and irritated by my companions. I also knew with equal certainty that when this happened the fault would be mine, not theirs.

During the night a fox barked somewhere on the slopes above us. At dawn al Auf untied the camels, which he had brought in for the night, and turned them loose to graze. There would be no food till sunset, but bin Kabina heated what was left of the coffee. After we had travelled for an hour we came upon a patch of grazing freshened by a recent shower. Faced with the choice of pushing on or of feeding the camels al Auf decided to stop, and as we unloaded them he told us to collect bundles of tribulus to carry with us. I watched him scoop a hole in the sand to find out how deeply the rain had penetrated, in this case about three feet; he invariably did this wherever rain had fallen – if no plants had yet come up on which to graze the camels while we waited, we went on, leaving him behind to carry out his investigations. It was difficult to see what practical use this information about future grazing in the heart of the Empty Quarter could possibly be to him or to anyone else, and yet I realized that it was this sort of knowledge which made him such an exceptional guide. Later I lay on the sand and watched an eagle circling overhead. It was hot. I took the temperature in the shade of my body and found it was 84 degrees. It was difficult to believe that it had been down to 43 degrees at dawn. Already the sun had warmed the sand so that it burnt the soft skin round the sides of my feet.

At midday we went on, passing high, pale-coloured dunes, and others that were golden, and in the evening we wasted an hour skirting a great mountain of red sand, probably 650 feet in height. Beyond it we travelled along a salt-flat, which formed a corridor through the Sands. Looking back I fancied the great, red dune was a door which was slowly, silently closing behind us. I watched the narrowing gap between it and the dune on the other side of the corridor, and imagined that once it was shut we could never go back, whatever happened. The gap vanished and now I could see only a wall of sand. I turned back to the others and they were discussing the price of a coloured loin-cloth which Mabkhaut had bought in Salala before we started. Suddenly al Auf pointed to a camel's track and said, 'Those were made by my camel when I came this way on my way to Ghanim.'

Later Musallim and al Auf argued how far it was from Mughshin to Bai, where Tamtaim and the others were to wait for us. I asked al Auf if he had ever ridden from the Wadi al Amairi to Bai. He answered, 'Yes, six years ago.'

'How many days did it take?'

'I will tell you. We watered at al Ghaba in the Amairi. There were four of us, myself, Salim, Janazil of the Awamir, and Alaiwi of the Afar; it was in the middle of summer. We had been to Ibri to settle the feud between the Rashid and the Mahamid, started by the killing of Fahad's son.'

Musallim interrupted, 'That must have been before the Riqaishi was Governor of Ibri. I had been there myself the year before. Sahail was with me and we went there from . . .'

But al Auf went on, 'I was riding the three-year-old I had bought from bin Duailan.'

'The one the Manahil raided from the Yam?' Bin Kabina asked.

'Yes. I exchanged it later for the yellow six-year-old I got from bin Ham. Janazil rode a Batina camel. Do you remember her? She was the daughter of the famous grey which belonged to Harahaish of the Wahiba.'

Mabkhaut said, 'Yes, I saw her last year when he was in Salala, a tall animal; she was old when I saw her, past her prime but even then a real beauty.'

Al Auf went on, 'We spent the night with Rai of the Afar.'

Bin Kabina chimed in, 'I met him last year when he came to Habarut; he carried a rifle, "a father of ten shots", which he had taken from the Mahra he had killed in the Ghudun. Bin Mautlauq offered him the grey yearling, the daughter of Farha, and fifty *riyals* for this rifle, but he refused.'

Al Auf continued, 'Rai killed a goat for our dinner and told us . . .', but I interrupted: 'Yes, but how many days did it take you to get to Bai?' He looked at me in surprise and said, 'Am I not telling you?'

We stopped at sunset for the evening meal, and fed to our camels the tribulus we had brought with us. All the skins were sweating and we were worried about our water. There had been a regular and ominous drip from them throughout the day, a drop falling on to the sand every few yards as we rode along, like blood dripping from a wound that could not be staunched. There was nothing to do but to press on, and yet to push the camels too hard would be to founder them. They were already showing signs of thirst. Al Auf had decided to go on again after we had fed, and while Musallim and bin Kabina baked bread I asked him about his former journeys through these Sands. 'I have crossed them

9

twice,' he said. 'The last time I came this way was two years ago. I was coming from Abu Dhabi.' I asked, 'Who was with you?' and he answered, 'I was alone.' Thinking that I must have misunderstood him, I repeated, 'Who were your companions?' 'God was my companion.' To have ridden alone through this appalling desolation was an incredible achievement. We were travelling through it now, but we carried our own world with us: a small world of five people, which yet provided each of us with companionship, with talk and laughter and the knowledge that others were there to share the hardship and the danger. I knew that if I travelled here alone the weight of this vast solitude would crush me utterly.

I also knew that al Auf had used no figure of speech when he said that God was his companion. To these Bedu, God is a reality, and the conviction of his presence gives them the courage to endure. For them to doubt his existence would be as inconceivable as for them to blaspheme. Most of them pray regularly, and many keep the fast of Ramadhan, which lasts for a whole month during which time a man may not eat or drink from dawn till sunset. When this fast falls in summer – and the Arab months being lunar it is eleven days earlier each year – they make use of the exemption which allows travellers to observe the fast when they have finished their journey, and keep it in the winter. Several of the Arabs whom we had left at Mughshin were fasting to compensate for not having done so earlier in the year. I have heard townsmen and villagers in the Hadhramaut and the Hajaz disparage the Bedu, as being without religion. When I have protested, they have said, 'Even if they pray, their prayers are not acceptable to God, since they do not first perform the proper ablutions.'

These Bedu are not fanatical. Once I was travelling with a large party of Rashid, one of whom said to me, 'Why don't you become a Muslim and then you would really be one of us?' I answered, 'God protect me from the Devil!' They laughed. This invocation is one which Arabs invariably use in rejecting something shameful or indecent. I would not have dared to make it if other Arabs had asked me this question, but the man who had spoken would certainly have used it if I had suggested that he should become a Christian.

After the meal we rode for two hours along a salt-flat. The dunes on either side, colourless in the moonlight, seemed higher by night than by day. The lighted slopes looked very smooth, the shadows in their folds inky black. Soon I was shivering uncontrollably from the cold. The others roared out their songs into a silence, broken otherwise only by the crunch of salt beneath the camels' feet. The words were the words of the south, but the rhythm and intonation were the same as in the songs which I had heard other Bedu singing in the Syrian desert. At first sight the Bedu of southern Arabia had appeared to be very different from those of the north, but I now realized that this difference was largely superficial and due to the clothes which they wore. My companions would not have felt out of place in an encampment of the Rualla, whereas a townsman from Aden or Muscat would be conspicuous in Damascus.

Eventually we halted and I dismounted numbly. I would have given much for a hot drink but I knew that I must wait eighteen hours for that. We lit a small fire and warmed ourselves before we slept, though I slept little. I was tired; for days I had ridden long hours on a rough camel, my body racked by its uneven gait. I suppose I was weak from hunger, for the food which we ate was a starvation ration, even by Bedu standards. But my thirst troubled me most; it was not bad enough really to distress me but I was always conscious of it. Even when I was asleep I dreamt of racing streams of ice-cold water, but it was difficult to get to sleep. Now I lay there trying to estimate the distance we had covered and the distance that still lay ahead. When I had asked al Auf how far it was to the well, he had answered, 'It is not the distance but the great dunes of the Uruq al Shaiba that may destroy us.' I worried about the water which I had watched dripping away on to the sand, and about the state of our camels. They were there, close beside me in the dark. I sat up and looked at them. Mabkhaut stirred and called out, 'What is it, Umbarak?' I mumbled an answer and lay down again. Then I worried whether we had tied the mouth of the skin properly when we had last drawn water and wondered what would happen if one of us was sick or had an accident. It was easy to banish these thoughts in daylight, less easy in the lonely darkness. Then I thought of al Auf travelling here alone and felt ashamed.

The others were awake at the first light, anxious to push on while it was still cold. The camels sniffed at the withered tribulus but were too thirsty to eat it. In a few minutes we were ready. We plodded along in silence. My eyes watered with the cold; the jagged salt-crusts cut and stung my feet. The world was grey and dreary. Then gradually the peaks ahead of us stood out against a paling sky; almost imperceptibly they began to glow, borrowing the colours of the sunrise which touched their crests.

A high unbroken dune-chain stretched across our front. It was not of uniform height, but, like a mountain range, consisted of peaks and connecting passes. Several of the summits appeared to be seven hundred feet above the salt-flat on which we stood. The southern face confronting us was very steep, which meant that this was the lee side to the prevailing winds. I wished we had to climb it from the opposite direction, for it is easy to take a camel down these precipices of sand but always difficult to find a way up them.

Al Auf told us to wait while he went to reconnoitre. I watched him walking away across the glistening salt-flat, his rifle on his shoulder and his head thrown back as he scanned the slopes above. He looked superbly confident, but as I viewed this wall of sand I despaired that we would ever get the camels up it. Mabkhaut evidently thought the same, for he said to Musallim, 'We will have to find a way round. No camel will ever climb that.' Musallim answered, 'It is al Auf's doing. He brought us here. We should have gone much farther to the west, nearer to Dakaka.' He had caught a cold and was snuffling, and his rather high-pitched voice was hoarse and edged with grievance. I knew that he was jealous of al Auf and always ready to disparage him, so unwisely I gibed, 'We should have got a long way if you had been our guide!' He swung round and answered angrily, 'You don't like the Bait Kathir. I know that you only like the Rashid. I defied my tribe to bring you here and you never recognize what I have done for you.'

For the past few days he had taken every opportunity of reminding me that I could not have come on from Ramlat al Ghafa without him. It was done in the hope of currying favour and of increasing his reward, but it only irritated me. Now I was tempted to seek relief in angry words, to welcome the silly, bitter squabble which would result. I kept silent with an effort and moved apart on the excuse of taking a photograph. I knew how easily, under conditions such as these, I could take a violent dislike to one member of the party and use him as my private scapegoat. I thought, 'I must not let myself dislike him. After all, I do owe him a great deal; but I wish to God he would not go on reminding me of it.'

I went over to a bank and sat down to wait for al Auf's return. The ground was still cold, although the sun was now well up, throwing a hard, clear light on the barrier of sand ahead of us. It seemed fantastic that this great rampart which shut out half the sky could be made of wind-blown sand. Now I could see al Auf, about half a mile away, moving along the salt-flat at the bottom of the dune. While I watched him he started to climb a ridge, like a mountaineer struggling upward through soft snow towards a pass over a high mountain. I even saw the tracks which he left behind him. He was the only moving thing in all that empty, silent landscape.

What were we going to do if we could not get the camels over it? I knew that we could not go any farther to the east, for al Auf had told me that the quicksands of Umm al Samim were in that direction. To the west the easier sands of Dakaka, where Thomas had crossed, were more than two hundred miles away. We had no margin, and could not afford to lengthen our journey. Our water was already dangerously short, and even more urgent than our own needs were those of the camels, which would collapse unless they were watered soon. We *must* get them over this monstrous dune, if necessary by unloading them and carrying the loads to the top. But what was on the other side? How many more of these dunes were there ahead of us? If we turned back now we might reach Mughshin, but I knew that once we crossed this dune the camels would be too tired and thirsty to get back even to Ghanim. Then I thought of Sultan and the others who had deserted us, and of their triumph if we gave up and returned defeated. Looking again at the dune ahead I noticed that al Auf was coming back. A shadow fell across the sand beside me. I glanced up and bin Kabina stood there. He smiled, said 'Salam Alaikum', and sat down. Urgently I turned to him and asked, 'Will we ever get the camels over that?' He pushed the hair back from his forehead, looked thoughtfully at the slopes above us, and answered, 'It is very steep but al Auf will find a way. He is a Rashid; he is not like these Bait Kathir.' Unconcernedly he then took the bolt out of his rifle and began to clean it with the hem of his shirt, while he asked me if all the English used the same kind of rifle.

When al Auf approached we went over to the others. Mabkhaut's camel had lain down; the rest of them stood where we had left them, which was a bad sign. Ordinarily they would have roamed off at once to look for food. Al Auf smiled at me as he came up but said nothing, and no one questioned him. Noticing that my camel's load was unbalanced he heaved up the saddle-bag from one side, and then picking up with his toes the camel-stick which he had dropped, he went over to his own camel, caught hold of its head-rope, said 'Come on', and led us forward.

It was now that he really showed his skill. He picked his way unerringly, choosing the inclines up which the camels could climb. Here on the lee side of this range a succession of great faces flowed down in unruffled sheets of sand, from the top to the very bottom of the dune. They were unscalable, for the sand was poised always on the verge of avalanching, but they were flanked by ridges where the sand was firmer and the inclines easier. It was possible to force a circuitous way up these slopes, but not all were practicable for camels, and from below it was difficult to judge their steepness. Very slowly, a foot at a time, we coaxed the unwilling beasts upward. Each time we stopped I looked up at the crests where the rising wind was blowing streamers of sand into the void, and wondered how we should ever reach the top. Suddenly we were there. Before slumping down on the sand I looked anxiously ahead of us. To my relief I saw that we were on the edge of rolling downs, where the going would be easy among shallow valleys and low, rounded hills. 'We have made it. We are on top of Uruq al Shaiba', I thought triumphantly. The fear of this great obstacle had lain like a shadow on my mind ever since al Auf had first warned me of it, the night we spoke together in the sands of Ghanim. Now the shadow had lifted and I was confident of success.

We rested for a while on the sand, not troubling to talk, until al Auf rose to his feet and said 'Come on'. Some small dunes built up by cross-winds ran in curves parallel with the main face across the back of these downs. Their steep faces were to the north and the camels slithered down them without difficulty. These downs were brick-red, splashed with deeper shades of colour; the underlying sand, exposed where it had been churned up by our feet, showing red of a paler shade. But the most curious feature was a number of deep craters resembling giant hoof-prints. These were unlike normal crescent-dunes, since they did not rise above their surroundings, but formed hollows in the floor of hard undulating sand. The salt-flats far below us looked very white.

We mounted our camels. My companions had muffled their faces in their head-cloths and rode in silence, swaying to the camels' stride. The shadows on the sand were very blue, of the same tone as the sky;

two ravens flew northward, croaking as they passed. I struggled to keep awake. The only sound was made by the slap of the camels' feet, like wavelets lapping on a beach.

To rest the camels we stopped for four hours in the late afternoon on a long gentle slope which stretched down to another salt-flat. There was no vegetation on it and no salt-bushes bordered the plain below us. Al Auf announced that we would go on again at sunset. While we were feeding I said to him cheerfully, 'Anyway, the worst should be over now that we are across the Uruq al Shaiba.' He looked at me for a moment and then answered, 'If we go well tonight we should reach them tomorrow.' I said, 'Reach what?' and he replied, 'The Uruq al Shaiba', adding, 'Did you think what we crossed today was the Uruq al Shaiba? That was only a dune. You will see them tomorrow.' For a moment, I thought he was joking, and then I realized that he was serious, that the worst of the journey which I had thought was behind us was still ahead.

It was midnight when at last al Auf said, 'Let's stop here. We will get some sleep and give the camels a rest. The Uruq al Shaiba are not far away now.' In my dreams that night they towered above us higher than the Himalayas.

Al Auf woke us again while it was still dark. As usual bin Kabina made coffee, and the sharp-tasting drops which he poured out stimulated but did not warm. The morning star had risen above the dunes. Formless things regained their shape in the first dim light of dawn. The grunting camels heaved themselves erect. We lingered for a moment more beside the fire; then al Auf said 'Come', and we moved forward. Beneath my feet the gritty sand was cold as frozen snow.

We were faced by a range as high as, perhaps even higher than, the range we had crossed the day before, but here the peaks were steeper and more pronounced, rising in many cases to great pinnacles, down which the flowing ridges swept like draperies. These sands, paler coloured than those we had crossed, were very soft, cascading round our feet as the camels struggled up the slopes. Remembering how little warning of imminent collapse the dying camels had given me twelve years before in the Danakil country, I wondered how much more these camels would stand, for they were trembling violently whenever they halted. When one refused to go on we heaved on her head-rope, pushed her from behind, and lifted the loads on either side as we manhandled the roaring animal upward. Sometimes one of them lay down and refused to rise, and then we had to unload her, and carry the water-skins and the saddlebags ourselves. Not that the loads were heavy. We had only a few gallons of water left and some handfuls of flour.

We led the trembling, hesitating animals upward along great sweeping ridges where the knife-edged crests crumbled beneath our feet! Although it was killing work, my companions were always gentle and infinitely patient. The sun was scorching hot and I felt empty, sick, and dizzy. As I struggled up the slope, knee-deep in shifting sand, my heart thumped wildly and my thirst grew worse. I found it difficult to swallow; even my ears felt blocked, and yet I knew that it would be many intolerable hours before I could drink. I would stop to rest, dropping down on the scorching sand, and immediately it seemed I would hear the others shouting, 'Umbarak, Umbarak'; their voices sounded strained and hoarse.

It took us three hours to cross this range.

On the summit were no gently undulating downs such as we had met the day before. Instead three smaller dune-chains rode upon its back, and beyond them the sand fell away to a salt-flat in another great empty trough between the mountains. The range on the far side seemed even higher than the one on which we stood, and behind it were others. I looked round, seeking instinctively for some escape. There was no limit to my vision. Somewhere in the ultimate distance the sands merged into the sky, but in that infinity of space I could see no living thing, not even a withered plant to give me hope. 'There is nowhere to go', I thought. 'We cannot go back and our camels will never get up another of these awful dunes. We really are finished.' The silence flowed over me, drowning the voices of my companions and the fidgeting of their camels.

We went down into the valley, and somehow – and I shall never know how the camels did it – we got up the other side. There, utterly exhausted, we collapsed. Al Auf gave us each a little water, enough to wet our mouths. He said, 'We need this if we are to go on.' The midday sun had drained the colour from the sands.

Scattered banks of cumulus cloud threw shadows across the dunes and salt-flats, and added an illusion that we were high among Alpine peaks, with frozen lakes of blue and green in the valley, far below. Half asleep, I turned over, but the sand burnt through my shirt and woke me from my dreams.

Two hours later al Auf roused us. As he helped me load my camel, he said, 'Cheer up, Umbarak. This time we really are across the Uruq al Shaiba', and when I pointed to the ranges ahead of us, he answered, 'I can find a way through those; we need not cross them.' We went on till sunset, but we were going with the grain of the country, following the valleys and no longer trying to climb the dunes. We should not have been able to cross another. There was a little fresh *qassis* on the slope where we halted. I hoped that this lucky find would give us an excuse to stop here for the night, but, after we had fed, al Auf went to fetch the camels, saying, 'We must go on again while it is cool if we are ever to reach Dhafara.'

We stopped long after midnight and started again at dawn, still exhausted from the strain and long hours of yesterday, but al Auf encouraged us by saying that the worst was over. The dunes were certainly lower than they had been, more uniform in height and more rounded, with fewer peaks. Four hours after we had started we came to rolling uplands of gold and silver sand, but still there was nothing for the camels to eat.

A hare jumped out from under a bush, and al Auf knocked it over with his stick. The others shouted 'God has given us meat.' For days we had talked of food; every conversation seemed to lead back to it. Since we had left Ghanim I had been always conscious of the dull ache of hunger, yet in the evening my throat was dry even after my drink, so that I found it difficult to swallow the dry bread Musallim set before us. All day we thought and talked about that hare, and by three o'clock in the afternoon could no longer resist stopping to cook it. Mabkhaut suggested, 'Let's roast it in its skin in the embers of a fire. That will save our water – we haven't got much left.' Bin Kabina led the chorus of protest. 'No, by God! Don't even suggest such a thing'; and turning to me he said, 'We don't want Mabkhaut's charred meat. Soup. We want soup and extra bread. We will feed well today even if we go hungry and thirsty later. By God, I am hungry!' We agreed to make soup. We were across the Uruq al Shaiba and intended to celebrate our achievement with this gift from God. Unless our camels foundered we were safe; even if our water ran out we should live to reach a well.

Musallim made nearly double our usual quantity of bread while bin Kabina cooked the hare. He looked across at me and said. 'The smell of this meat makes me faint.' When it was ready he divided it into five portions. They were very small, for an Arabian hare is no larger than an English rabbit, and this one was not even fully grown. Al Auf named the lots and Mabkhaut drew them. Each of us took the small pile of meat which had fallen to him. Then bin Kabina said, 'God! I have forgotten to divide the liver', and the others said, 'Give it to Umbarak.' I protested, saying that they

22

should divide it, but they swore by God that they would not eat it and that I was to have it. Eventually I took it, knowing that I ought not, but too greedy for this extra scrap of meat to care.

Our water was nearly finished and there was only enough flour for about another week. The starving camels were so thirsty that they had refused to eat some half-dried herbage which we had passed. We must water them in the next day or two or they would collapse. Al Auf said that it would take us three more days to reach Khaba well in Dhafara, but that there was a very brackish well not far away. He thought that the camels might drink its water.

That night after we had ridden for a little over an hour it grew suddenly dark. Thinking that a cloud must be covering the full moon, I looked over my shoulder and saw that there was an eclipse and that half the moon was already obscured. Bin Kabina noticed it at the same moment and broke into a chant which the others took up.

> God endures for ever.
> The life of man is short.
> The Pleiades are overhead.
> The moon's among the stars.

Otherwise they paid no attention to the eclipse (which was total), but looked around for a place to camp.

We started very early the next morning and rode without a stop for seven hours across easy rolling downs. The colour of these sands was vivid, varied, and unexpected: in places the colour of ground coffee, elsewhere brick-red, or purple, or a curious golden-green. There were small white gypsum-flats, fringed with *shanan*, a grey-green salt-bush, lying in hollows in the downs. We rested for two hours on sands the colour of dried blood and then led our camels on again.

Suddenly we were challenged by an Arab lying behind a bush on the crest of a dune. Our rifles were on our camels, for we had not expected to meet anyone here. Musallim was hidden behind mine. I watched him draw his rifle clear. But al Auf said, 'It is the voice of a Rashid', and walked forward. He spoke to the concealed Arab, who rose and came to meet him. They embraced and stood talking until we joined them. We greeted the man, and al Auf said, 'This is Hamad bin Hanna, a sheikh of the Rashid.' He was a heavily-built bearded man of middle age. His eyes were set close together and he had a long nose with a blunt end. He fetched his camel from behind the dune while we unloaded.

We made coffee for him and listened to his news. He told us that he had been looking for a stray camel when he crossed our tracks and had taken us for a raiding party from the south. Ibn Saud's tax-collectors were in Dhafara and the Rabadh, collecting tribute from the tribes; and there were Rashid, Awamir, Murra, and some Manahil to the north of us.

We had to avoid all contact with Arabs other than the Rashid, and if possible even with them, so that news of my presence would not get about among the tribes, for I had no desire to be arrested by Ibn Saud's tax-collectors and taken off to explain my presence here to Ibn Jalawi, the formidable Governor of the Hasa. Karab from the Hadhramaut had raided these sands the year before, so there was also a serious risk of our being mistaken for raiders, since the tracks of our camels would show that we had come from the southern steppes. This risk would be increased if it appeared that we were avoiding the Arabs, for honest travellers never pass an encampment without seeking news and food. It was going to be very difficult to escape detection. First we must water our camels and draw water for ourselves. Then we must lie up as close as possible to Liwa and send a party to the villages to buy us enough food for at least another month. Hamad told me that Liwa belonged to the Al bu Falah of Abu Dhabi. He said that they were still fighting Said bin Maktum of Dibai, and that, as there was a lot of raiding going on, the Arabs would be very much on the alert.

We started again in the late afternoon and travelled till sunset. Hamad came with us and said he would stay with us until we had got food from Liwa. Knowing where the Arabs were encamped he could help us to avoid them. Next day, after seven hours' travelling, we reached Khaur Sabakha on the edge of the Dhafara sands. We cleaned out the well and found brackish water at seven feet, so bitter that even the camels only drank a little before refusing it. They sniffed thirstily at the water with which al Auf tried to coax them from a leather bucket, but only dipped their lips into it. We covered their noses but still they would not drink. Yet al Auf said that Arabs themselves drank this water mixed with milk, and when I expressed my disbelief he added that if an Arab was really thirsty he would even kill a camel and drink the liquid in its stomach, or ram a stick down its throat and drink the vomit. We went on again till nearly sunset.

The next day when we halted in the afternoon al Auf told us we had reached Dhafara and that Khaba well was close. He said that he would fetch water in the morning. We finished what little was left in one of our skins. Next day we remained where we were. Hamad said that he would go for news and return the following day. Al Auf, who went with him, came back in the afternoon with two skins full of water which, although slightly brackish, was delicious after the filthy evil-smelling dregs we had drunk the night before.

It was 12 December, fourteen days since we had left Khaur bin Atarit in Ghanim.

In the evening, now that we needed no longer measure out each cup of water, bin Kabina made extra coffee, while Musallim increased our rations of flour by a mugful. This was wild extravagance, but we felt that the occasion called for celebration. Even so, the loaves he handed us were woefully inadequate to stay our hunger, now that our thirst was gone.

The moon was high above us when I lay down to sleep. The others still talked round the fire, but I closed my mind to the meaning of their words, content to hear only the murmur of their voices, to watch their outlines sharp against the sky, happily conscious that they were there and beyond them the camels to which we owed our lives.

For years the Empty Quarter had represented to me the final, unattainable challenge which the desert offered. Suddenly it had come within my reach. I remembered my excitement when Lean had casually offered me the chance to go there, the immediate determination to cross it, and then the doubts and fears, the frustrations, and the moments of despair. Now I had crossed it. To others my journey would have little importance. It would produce nothing except a rather inaccurate map which no one was ever likely to use. It was a personal experience, and the reward had been a drink of clean, nearly tasteless water. I was content with that.

Looking back on the journey I realized that there had been no high moment of achievement such as a mountaineer must feel when he stands upon his chosen summit. Over the past days new strains and anxieties had built up as others eased, for, after all, this crossing of the Empty Quarter was set in the framework of a longer journey, and already my mind was busy with the new problems which our return journey presented.

Return to Salala

We were across the Empty Quarter, but we still had to return to Salala. We could not go back the way we had come. The only possible route was through Oman.

I tried to work out our position on a map which showed Mughshin and Abu Dhabi but nothing else, except from hearsay. It was difficult to plot our course with no firm surface larger than my notebook on which to work. Bin Kabina held the map while the others sat and watched, and all of them distracted me with questions. They could never follow a map unless it was orientated, though curiously enough they could understand a photograph even when they held it upside down. I estimated that we should have between five hundred and six hundred miles to travel before we could rejoin Tamtaim and the rest of the Bait Kathir on the southern coast, and then a further two hundred miles to reach Salala. I asked al Auf about water and he said, 'Don't worry about that, there are plenty of wells ahead of us. It is food which is going to be our trouble.' We went over to the saddle-bags and Musallim measured out the flour. There were nine mugfuls left – about seven pounds.

While we were doing this, Hamad came back, bringing with him another Rashid, called Jadid. 'Another mouth to feed', I thought as soon as I saw him. Bin

Kabina made coffee for them, and we then discussed our plans. Hamad assured us that we should be able to buy plenty of food in Liwa, enlarging on what we should find there – flour and rice and dates and coffee and sugar – but he added that it would take us three, perhaps four, days to get there. I said wryly, 'We shall be as hungry as the camels', and al Auf grunted, 'Yes, but the sons of Adam cannot endure like camels.' Hamad, questioned by Mabkhaut and Mussalim, said that as long as we remained to the south of Liwa we should be outside the range of the fighting on the coast, and insisted that all the tribes in the south, whether they were Awamir, Manasir, or Bani Yas, were on good terms with the Rashid. He said, 'It will be different when you reach Oman. There the Duru are our enemies. There is no good in any of the Duru. You will have to be careful while you are among them for they are a treacherous race.' Al Auf laughed and quoted, 'He died of snake-bite', a well-known expression for Duru treachery.

He was tracing patterns on the sand with his camel-stick, smoothing them out and starting again. He looked up and said thoughtfully; 'The difficulty is Umbarak. No one must know he is here. If the Arabs hear that there is a Christian in the sands they will talk of nothing else, and the news will soon be all round the place. Then Ibn Saud's tax-collectors will hear of it and they will arrest us all and take us off to Ibn Jalawi in the Hasa. God preserve us from that. I know Ibn Jalawi. He is a tyrant, utterly without mercy. Anyway, we don't want the news about Umbarak to get ahead of us among the Duru. We shall never get through the country if it does. If we meet any Arabs we had better say that we are Rashid from the Hadhramaut, travelling to Abu Dhabi to fight for the Al bu Falah. Umbarak can be an Arab from Aden.'

Turning to me, he said, 'Keep quiet if we meet anyone. Just answer their salutations, and, what is more, from now on you must ride all the time. Any Arab who came across your monstrous footprints would certainly follow them to find out who on earth you were.' He got up to fetch the camel, saying, 'We had better be off.'

We went down to Khaba well. It was three miles away in a bare hollow, among a jumble of small, white crescent-dunes. The water was ten feet below the surface, and it took us a long time to water the camels, for we had only one small leather bucket, and each camel drank ten to twelve gallons. Bin Kabina stood beside Qamaiqam and whenever she stopped he scratched between her hind legs and crooned endearments to encourage her to drink again. At last all of them were satisfied, blown out with the water which they had sucked up in long slow draughts. Al Auf dashed a few bucketfuls against their chests, and then started to fill the water-skins. The sun was very hot before we had finished. We mounted. My companions had wrapped themselves in their cloaks and muffled their faces in their head-cloths till only their eyes showed. I remembered a Bedu I had once seen in Syria. It was noon on a blazing midsummer day and he was trudging across the desert, travelling apparently from nowhere to nowhere, enveloped to his feet in a heavy sheepskin coat. Arabs argue that the extra clothes which they put on when it is hot keep the heat out; in fact, what they do is to stop the sweat from evaporating and thereby build up a cool layer of air next to the skin. I could never bear this clammy discomfort and preferred to lose moisture by letting the hot air dry my skin. But if I had done this in summer I should have died of heat-stroke.

Next day we had difficulty in avoiding several inquisitive Awamir, who at first took us for raiders and gave the alarm. Hamad got in touch with them and said that we were a party of Rashid going to Abu Dhabi. They then invited us to their encampment, saying that they would slaughter a camel for us. Hamad made excuses and this again aroused their suspicions, but when we camped Hamad, al Auf, and Mabkhaut went back to their encampment and spent the night there in order to reassure them. When they returned in the morning they brought us a goatskin full of milk. Three days after leaving Khaba we reached the Batin, and lay up in the dunes near Balagh well. Next morning Hamad, Jadid, and bin Kabina went to the settlements in Liwa to buy food. They took three camels with them, and I told bin Kabina to buy flour, sugar, tea, coffee, butter, dates, and rice if he could get any, and above all to bring back a goat. Our flour was finished, but that evening Musallim produced from his saddle-bags a few handfuls of maize, which we roasted and ate. It was to be the last food we had until the others returned from Liwa three days later. They were three interminable nights and days.

I had almost persuaded myself that I was con-ditioned to starvation, indifferent to it. After all, I had been hungry for weeks, and even when we had had flour I had had little inclination to eat the charred or sodden lumps which Musallim had cooked. I used to swallow my portion with even less satisfaction than that with which I eventually avoided it. Certainly I thought and talked incessantly of food, but as a prisoner talks of freedom, for I realized that the joints of meat, the piles of rice, and the bowls of steaming gravy which tantalized me could have no reality outside my mind. I had never thought then that I should dream of the crusts which I was rejecting.

For the first day my hunger was only a more insistent feeling of familiar emptiness; something which, like a toothache, I could partly overcome by an effort of will. I woke in the grey dawn craving for food, but by lying on my stomach and pressing down I could achieve a semblance of relief. At least I was warm. Later, as the sun rose, the heat forced me out of my sleeping-bag. I threw my cloak over a bush and lay in the shade and tried to sleep again. I dozed and dreamt of food; I woke and thought of food. I tried to read, but it was difficult to concentrate. A moment's slackness and I was thinking once more of food. I filled myself with water, and the bitter water, which I did not want, made me feel sick. Eventually it was evening and we gathered round the fire, repeating, 'Tomorrow they will be back';

and thought of the supplies of food which bin Kabina would bring with him, and of the goat which we should eat. But the next day dragged out till sunset, and they did not come.

I faced another night, and the nights were worse than the days. Now I was cold and could not even sleep, except in snatches. I watched the stars; some of them – Orion, the Pleiades, and the Bear – I knew by name, others only by sight. Slowly they swung overhead and dipped down towards the west, while the bitter wind keened among the dunes. I remembered how I had once awakened with hunger during my first term at school and cried, remembering some chocolate cake which I had been too gorged to eat when my mother had taken me out to tea two days before. Now I was maddened by the thought of the crusts which I had given away in the Uruq al Shaiba. Why had I been such a fool? I could picture the colour and texture, even the shape, of the fragments which I had left.

In the morning I watched Mabkhaut turn the camels out to graze, and as they shuffled off, spared for a while from the toil which we imposed upon them, I found that I could only think of them as food. I was glad when they were out of sight. Al Auf came over and lay down near me, covering himself with his cloak; I don't think we spoke. I lay with my eyes shut, insisting to myself, 'If I were in London I would give anything to be here.' Then I thought of the jeeps and lorries with which the Locust Officers in the Najd were equipped. So vivid were my thoughts that I could hear the engines, smell the stink of petrol fumes. No, I would rather be here starving as I was than sitting in a chair, replete with food, listening to the wireless, and dependent upon cars to take me through Arabia. I clung desperately to this conviction. It seemed infinitely important. Even to doubt it was to admit defeat, to forswear everything to which I held.

I dozed and heard a camel roaring. I jerked awake, thinking, 'They have come at last', but it was only Mabkhaut moving our camels. The shadows lengthened among the sand-hills; the sun had set and we had given up hope when they returned. I saw at once that they had no goat with them. My dream of a large hot stew vanished. We exchanged the formal greetings and asked the formal questions about the news. Then we helped them with the only camel which was loaded. Bin Kabina said wearily, 'We got nothing. There is nothing to be had in Liwa. We have two packages of bad dates and a little wheat. They would not take our *riyals* – they wanted rupees. At last they took them at the same valuation as rupees, God's curse on them!' He had run a long palm-splinter into his foot and was limping. I tried to get it out but it was already too dark to see.

We opened a package of dates and ate. They were of poor quality and coated with sand, but there were plenty of them. Later we made porridge from the wheat, squeezing some dates into it to give it a flavour. After we had fed, al Auf said, 'If this is all we are going to have we shall soon be too weak to get on our camels.' We were a depressed and ill-tempered party that evening.

The past three days had been an ordeal, worse for the others than for me, since, but for me, they could have ridden to the nearest tents and fed. However, we had not suffered the final agony of doubt. We had known that the others would return and bring us food. We had thought of this food, talked of this food, dreamt of this food. A feast of rich and savoury meat, the reward of our endurance. Now all we had was this. Some wizened dates, coated with sand, and a mess of boiled grain. There was not even enough of it. We had to get back across Arabia, travelling secretly, and we had enough food for ten days if we were economical. I had eaten tonight, but I was starving. I wondered how much longer I should be able to face this fare. We *must* get more food. Al Auf said, 'We must get hold of a camel and eat that', and I thought of living for a month on sun-dried camel's meat and nothing else. Hamad suggested that we should lie up near Ibri in the Wadi el Ain, and send a party into Ibri to buy food. He said, 'It is one of the biggest towns in Oman. You will get everything you want there.' With difficulty I refrained from pointing out that he had said this of Liwa.

Musallim interrupted and said that we could not possibly go into the Duru country; the Duru had heard about my visit to Mughshin last year and had warned the Bait Kathir not to bring any Christians into their territory. Al Auf asked him impatiently where in that case he did propose to go. They started to wrangle. I joined in and reminded Musallim that we had always planned to return through the Duru country. Excitedly he turned towards me and, flogging the ground with

35

his camel-stick to give emphasis to his words, shouted: 'Go through it? Yes, if we must, quickly and secretly, but through the uninhabited country near the sands. We never agreed to hang about in the Duru country, nor to go near Ibri. By God, it is madness! Don't you know that there is one of the Imam's governors there. He is the Riqaishi. Have you never heard of the Riqaishi? What do you suppose he will do if he hears there is a Christian in his country? He hates all infidels. I have been there. Listen, Umbarak, I know him. God help you, Umbarak, if he gets hold of you. Don't think that Oman is like the desert here. It is a settled country – villages and towns, and the Imam rules it all through his governors, and the worst of them all is the Riqaishi. The Duru, yes; Bedu like ourselves; our enemies, but we might smuggle you quickly through their land. But hang about there – no; and to go near Ibri would be madness. Do you hear? The first people who saw you, Umbarak, would go straight off and tell the Riqaishi.'

Al Auf asked him quietly, 'What do you want to do?' and Musallim stormed, 'God, I don't know. I only know I am not going near Ibri.' I asked him if he wanted to return to Salala by the way we had come, and added, 'It will be great fun, with worn-out camels and no food.' He shouted back that it would not be worse than going to Ibri. Exasperated by this stupidity, al Auf turned away muttering 'There is no god but God', while Musallim and I continued to wrangle until Mabkhaut and Hamad intervened to calm us.

Eventually we agreed that we must get food from Ibri and that meanwhile we would buy a camel from the Rashid who were ahead of us in the Rabadh, so that we should have an extra camel with us to eat if we were in trouble. Hamad said, 'You must conceal the fact that Umbarak is a Christian.' Mabkhaut suggested that I should pretend that I was a *saiyid* from the Hadhramaut, since no one would ever mistake me for a Bedu. I protested, 'That is no good; as a *saiyid* I should get involved in religious discussions. I should certainly be expected to pray, which I don't know how to do; they would probably even expect me to lead their prayers. A nice mess I should make of that.' The others laughed and agreed that this suggestion would not work. I said, 'While we are in the sands here I had better be an Aden townsman who has been living with the tribes and is now on his way to Abu Dhabi. When we get to Oman I will say I am a Syrian who has been visiting Riyadh and that I am now on my way to Salala.' Bin Kabina asked, 'What is a Syrian?' and I said, 'If you don't know what a Syrian is I don't suppose the Duru will either. Certainly they will never have seen one.'

I then asked him about Liwa. He said: 'There are palms, good ones, and quite a lot of them on the dunes above the salt-flats. The houses are of mats and palm fronds. I never saw a mud house. The villagers were all either Manasir or Bani Yas, an unfriendly lot. One slave noticed at once that the pads under my camel's saddle were made of coconut fibre and not of palm fibre. He called out, "This boy is from the south. He does not belong to the same party as the other two. He is prob-ably with some raiders who are hiding somewhere and

37

has come in to get food for them. They would all have come in if they were honest men." I told them that I was with two other Rashid, who had come north to fight for Al bu Falah, and that one of them had fever and that the other had remained to look after him.'

Mabkhaut exclaimed, 'They are devils, these slaves; they notice everything.'

Bin Kabina went on: 'By God, I would like to lift some of their camels, not that the ones I saw were worth taking. They are a wretched crowd, these villagers, not like the people at Salala. Their women refused even to grind our corn. Bad luck to them. I had to borrow a grindstone and do it myself after dark.'

I knew that this was a woman's job and that he would have been ashamed to be seen doing it. I asked what he had been given to eat, and he laughed and said, 'Bread, dates, and a stew made from skinks.' He was always sickened by lizard-meat. This started a discussion on what was lawful food. Arabs never distinguished between what is eatable and what is not, but always between food which is lawful and food which is forbidden. No Muslim may eat pork, blood, or the flesh of an animal which has not had its throat cut while it was still alive. Most of them will not eat meat slaughtered by anyone other than a Muslim, or by a boy who is still uncircumcised, although in Syria Muslims will eat meat killed by a Christian or a Druze. Otherwise the definition of what is lawful varies endlessly and in every place, and usually bears little relation to reason. I asked if a fox was lawful food, and Hamad explained to me that sand foxes were, but mountain foxes were not. They agreed that eagles were lawful, but ravens were forbidden, unless they were eaten as medicine to cure stomach ache. Musallim said that the Duru ate the wild donkeys which lived in their country, and the others expressed incredulity and disgust. I said I would far rather eat a donkey than a wild cat, which al Auf had just declared was lawful meat. The differences which had arisen between us a short while ago were forgotten.

Among these people arguments frequently become impassioned, but usually the excitement dies away as quickly as it arises. Men who were screaming at each other, ready apparently to resort to violence, will sit happily together a short while later drinking coffee. As a rule Bedu do not nurse a grievance, but if they think that their personal honour has been slighted they immediately become vindictive, bent on vengeance. Strike a Bedu and he will kill you either then or later. It is easy for strangers to give offence without meaning to do so. I once put my hand on the back of bin Kabina's neck and he turned on me and asked furiously if I took him for a slave. I had no idea that I had done anything wrong.

In the morning our camp was enveloped in thick mist. I could just make out an *abal* bush less than twenty yards from where I lay; beyond it was a drifting whiteness, dank as sea fog. Suddenly, somewhere, a camel roared, indicating that a human being had approached it. I felt for my rifle and glanced round to see if anyone was missing. Bin Kabina was puffing at a smoking pile of sticks; Musallim was piling lumps of dates on a tray; Hamad and Jadid were praying; and I realized it must be Mabkhaut and al Auf with the camels. I got up. The cloak which had covered my sleeping bag was drenched. Each night for the past week we had had this soaking dew, the result of the northerly winds which carried the moisture inland from the Persian Gulf. I had noticed that in the southern Sands dew and morning mist coincided with a southerly wind off the Arabian Sea. I do not think that much dew falls in the Empty Quarter itself, but nearer the coast the dew must freshen the herbage. I was always astounded when al Auf maintained that dew burnt it up.

Hamad now volunteered to accompany us as far as Ibri, an offer which we gladly accepted since he knew the Sands and the present distribution of the tribes. He said that we had better keep along the southern edge of Liwa, where the country was at present empty. Normally the salt-flats south of Liwa were filled with camel herds belonging to the Manasir, but recently they had been raided by a force from Dibai and had suffered losses. Now most of the Manasir were assembled farther to the west. Hamad explained to me that the Manasir pastured their camels on salt-bushes, which made them very thirsty, so that they had to be watered three or even four times a day. In consequence they were tied to the neighbourhood of the wells. Salt-bushes were little affected by drought and provided abundant and permanent grazing on the flats around Liwa. Our own camels would not eat these bushes, and bin Kabina asked if we should find anything for them on our route. He said, 'The wretched animals don't deserve any more starvation. It has made me miserable to watch their suffering.' Hamad assured him that we should find enough for them during the next few days and plenty as soon as we reached Rabadh. We therefore agreed to his suggestion.

We ate some dates, and Jadid then went back while the rest of us set off in an easterly direction, the mist still thick about us. I hoped we should not stumble on some Arab encampment. The mist did not lift for another two hours.

The dunes ran from west to east so that we were travelling easily. They consisted of great massifs similar to the *qaid* which I had seen in Ghanim, but there they were linked together to form parallel dune chains about three hundred feet in height, the broad valleys between them being covered with bright-green salt-bushes. We passed several palm groves and a few small settlements of dilapidated huts made, as bin Kabina had described, from matting and palm fronds. They were all abandoned.

At midday, while we were eating more of our revolting dates, two Arabs accompanied by a saluki appeared on a distant dune. They stood and watched us, so al Auf went over to them. They shouted to him not to come any nearer, and when he called back that he wanted 'the news' they answered that they had none and wanted none of his and threatened that they would shoot if he came any closer. They watched us for a while and then made off.

We travelled slowly to rest our camels and reached

the Rabadh sands five days after leaving Balagh. Sometimes we saw camels. It did not seem to matter how far off they were; my companions were apparently always able to distinguish if they were in milk. They would say, 'There are camels', and point to some dots on a dune a mile or more away. After a further scrutiny they would agree that one or more were in milk. We would then ride over to them, for travellers in the desert may milk any camels they encounter. These camels were feeding on salt-bushes and gushes of liquid green excrement poured constantly down their hocks. Al Auf told me that camels which fed on salt-bushes always scoured like this, but that it did them no harm provided they had plenty of water. Certainly most of these looked in excellent condition.

Once we passed a dozen camels tended by a woman with two small children. Al Auf said, 'Let's get a drink', and we rode over to them. He jumped from his camel, greeted the woman, a wizened old thing bundled up in black cloth turned green with age, took the bowl which she handed him, and went towards the camels. She shrilled at her sons, 'Hurry! Hurry! Fetch the red one. Fetch the two-year-old. God take you, child! Hurry! Fetch the red one. Fetch the two-year-old. Welcome! Welcome! Welcome to the guests!' Al Auf handed us the bowl and in turn we squatted down to drink, for no Arab drinks standing, while the old woman asked us where we were going. We answered that we were going to fight for the Al bu Falah and she exclaimed, 'God give you victory!'

On another occasion we came upon a small encamp-

ment of Manasir. Hamad insisted that we must go
over to them, or we should arouse their suspicions since
they had already seen us. We were on foot at the time
and I suggested that they should leave the camels to
graze and that I should herd them until they returned.
After some argument they agreed. I knew that they
wanted milk, and I should have liked a drink myself,
but it seemed stupid to run the risk of detection. When
they returned, bin Kabina grinned whenever he looked
at me, so I asked him what the joke was. He said, 'The
Manasir gave us milk but insisted that we should fetch
you, saying, 'Why do you leave your companion without milk?' Al Auf explained that you were our slave,
but they still insisted that we should fetch you.' I knew
that among Bedu even a slave is considered as a travelling companion, entitled to the same treatment as the
rest of the party. Bin Kabina went on, 'Finally al Auf
said, "Oh! he is half-witted. Leave him where he is",
and the Manasir insisted no more.' Mabkhaut said,
'True, they said no more, but they looked at us a bit
oddly.'

Next morning while we were leading our camels
down a steep dune face I was suddenly conscious of
a low vibrant hum, which grew in volume until it
sounded as though an aeroplane were flying low over
our heads. The frightened camels plunged about, tug-
ging at their head-ropes and looking back at the slope
above us. The sound ceased when we reached the
bottom. This was 'the singing of the sands'. The Arabs
describe it as roaring, which is perhaps a more descrip-
tive word. During the five years that I was in these

parts I only heard it half a dozen times. It is caused, I think, by one layer of sand slipping over another. Once I was standing on a dunecrest and the sound started as soon as I stepped on to the steep face. I found on this occassion that I could start it or stop it at will by stepping on or off this slip-face.

Near Rabadh, Musallim suddenly jumped off his camel, pushed his arm into a shallow burrow, and pulled out a hare. I asked him how he knew it was there, and he said that he had seen its track going in and none coming out. The afternoon dragged on until we reached the expanse of small contiguous dunes which give these sands the name of Rabadh. There was adequate grazing, so we stopped on their edge. We decided to eat the rest of our flour, and Musallim conjured three onions and some spices out of his saddle-bags. We sat round in a hungry circle watching bin Kabina cooking the hare, and offering advice. Anticipation mounted, for it was more than a month since we had eaten meat, except for the hare that al Auf had killed near the Uruq al Shaiba. We sampled the soup and decided to let it stew just a little longer. Then bin Kabina looked up and groaned, 'God! Guests!'

Coming across the sands towards us were three Arabs. Hamad said, 'They are Bakhit, and Umbarak, and Salim, the children of Mia', and to me, 'They are Rashid.' We greeted them, asked the news, made coffee for them, and then Musallim and bin Kabina dished up the hare and the bread and set it before them, saying with every appearance of sincerity that they were our guests, that God had brought them, that today was a blessed day, and a number of similar remarks. They asked us to join them but we refused, repeating that they were our guests. I hoped that I did not look as murderous as I felt while I joined the others in assuring them that God had brought them on this auspicious occasion. When they had finished, bin Kabina put a sticky lump of dates in a dish and called us over to feed.

Feeling thoroughly ill-tempered I lay down to sleep, but this was impossible. The others, excited by this meeting with their fellow-tribesmen, talked incessantly within a few yards of my head. I wondered irritably why Bedu must always shout. Gradually I relaxed. I tried the old spell of asking myself, 'Would I really wish to be anywhere else?' and having decided that I would not, I felt better. I pondered on this desert hospitality and, compared it with our own. I remembered other encampments where I had slept, small tents on which I had happened in the Syrian desert and where I had spent the night. Gaunt men in rags and hungry-looking children had greeted me, and bade me welcome with the sonorous phrases of the desert. Later they had set a great dish before me, rice heaped round a sheep which they had slaughtered, over which my host poured liquid golden butter until it flowed down on to the sand; and when I had protested, saying, 'Enough! Enough!', had answered that I was a hundred times welcome. Their lavish hospitality had always made me uncomfortable, for I had known that as a result of it they would go hungry for days. Yet when

I left them they had almost convinced me that I had done them a kindness by staying with them.

My thoughts were interrupted by the raised voices of my companions. Bin Kabina was protesting passionately. I could see him gesticulating against the sky. I listened and, as I had expected, they were talking about money, the rights and wrongs of some ancient dispute about a few shillings which concerned none of them. I wondered if any other race was as avaricious as the Arabs, with such an intense love of money, and then I thought of bin Kabina giving away his only loin-cloth in Ramlat al Ghafa and wondered who, other than a Bedu, would have done that. It is characteristic of Bedu to do things by extremes, to be either wildly generous or unbelievably mean, very patient or almost hysterically excitable, to be incredibly brave or to panic for no apparent reason. Ascetic by nature, they derive satisfaction from the bare simplicity of their lives and scorn the amenities which others would judge essential. Although, on the rare occasions that offer, they eat enormously, I have never met a Bedu who was greedy. Continent for months on end, not one of them, even the most austere, would regard celibacy as a virtue. They want sons, and consider that women are provided by God for the satisfaction of men. Deliberately to refrain from using them would be not only unnatural but also ridiculous, and Bedu are very susceptible to ridicule. Yet an Arab will use his sister's name as his battle-cry, and Glubb has suggested that the medieval conception of chivalry came to Europe from the Arabs at the time of the Crusades. Bedu set great score by human dignity, and most of them would prefer to watch a man die rather than see him humiliated. Always reserved in front of strangers and accustomed on formal occasions to sit for hours motionless and in silence, they are a garrulous, lighthearted race. But, at the instigation of religious zealots, they can become uncompromisingly puritanical, quick to frown on all amusement, regarding song and music as a sin and laughter as unseemly. Probably no other people, either as a race or as individuals, combine so many conflicting qualities in such an extreme degree.

I was dimly conscious of their voices until nearly dawn.

In the morning Bakhit pressed us to come to his tent, saying, 'I will give you fat and meat', the conventional way of saying that he would kill a camel for us. We were tempted, for we were very hungry, but Hamad said that it would be wiser not to go there, for the sands in which Bakhit was camped were full of Arabs. We told Bakhit that we wished to buy a camel, and he said he would fetch one and meet us next day at an abandoned well farther to the east. He met us there a little before sunset. He had with him an old camel, a *hazmia*, black-coated and in good condition, which had been bred in the sands. There were long strips of skin hanging from the soles of her feet. Al Auf said she would not be able to travel far on the gravel plains in the Duru country, but Mabkhaut answered that we could take her along with us until her feet wore through and then kill her. We bought her after a little haggling.

The next morning we saw some tents, and Hamad

said, 'I don't know who they are', so we bore off to the right in order to pass wide of them; but a man came out from among them and ran across the sand towards us, shouting, 'Stop! Stop!' As he came near, Hamad said, 'It is all right. He is Salim, old Muhammad's son.' We greeted him and he said, 'Why do you pass by my tent? Come, I will give you fat and meat.' I protested instinctively, but he silenced me by saying, 'If you do not come to my tent I shall divorce my wife.' This was the divorce oath, which he was bound to obey if we refused. He took my camel's rein and led her towards the tents. An old man came forward and greeted us. He had a long white beard, kindly eyes, and a gentle voice. He walked very upright, as do all the Bedu. Hamad said, 'This is old Muhammad.' The two tents were very small, less than three yards long and four feet high, and were half-filled with saddles and other gear. An old woman, a younger woman, and three children, one of them a small naked child with a running nose and his thumb in his mouth, watched us as we unloaded. The women were dressed in dark-blue robes, and were unveiled. The younger one was very pretty. Salim called to al Auf and together they went off across the dunes. They came back later with a young camel, which they slaughtered behind the tents.

Meanwhile the old man had made coffee and set out dates for us to eat. Hamad said, 'He is the Christian.' The old man asked, 'Is he the Christian who travelled last year with bin al Kamam and the Rashid to the Hadhramaut?' and after Hamad had assented he turned to me and said, 'A thousand welcomes.' It had not

48

taken long for this news to arrive, although here we were near the Persian Gulf, far from the Hadhramaut; but I was not surprised. I knew how interested Bedu always are in 'the news', how concerned to get the latest information about their kinsmen, about raids and tribal movements and grazing. I knew from experience how far they would go out of their way to ask for news. I had realized that it was the chance of getting this as much as the craving for milk that had tantalized my companions during the past days when we had seen and avoided distant tents. They hated travelling through inhabited country without knowing exactly what was happening around them.

'What is "the news"?' It is the question which follows every encounter in the desert even between strangers. Given a chance the Bedu will gossip for hours, as they had done last night, and nothing is too trivial for them to recount. There is no reticence in the desert. If a man distinguishes himself he knows that his fame will be widespread; if he disgraces himself he knows that the story of his shame will inevitably be heard in every encampment. It is this fear of public opinion which enforces at all times the rigid conventions of the desert. The consciousness that they are always before an audience makes many of their actions theatrical. Glubb once told me of a Bedu sheikh who was known as 'The Host of the Wolves', because whenever he heard a wolf howl round his tent he ordered his son to take a goat out in the desert, saying he would have no one call on him for dinner in vain.

It was late in the afternoon when Salim spread a rug

in front of us, and placed on it a large tray covered with rice. He lifted joints of meat from the cauldron and put them on this, ladled soup over the rice, and finally tipped a dishful of butter over it. He then poured water over our outstretched hands. Old Muhammad invited us to eat, but refused our invitation to join us. He stood and watched us, saying, 'Eat! Eat! You are hungry. You are tired. You have come a long way. Eat!' He shouted to Salim to bring more butter, although we protested that there was enough already, and taking the dish from Salim's hand poured it over the rice. Gorged at last, we licked our fingers and rose together muttering 'God requite you.' We washed, using water. There was no need here to clean our fingers with sand, for the well was near by. Salim then handed us coffee and the bitter drops were welcome and clean-tasting after the greasy rice and cold lumps of fat which we had eaten. He and his father urged us to remain with them at least for another day to rest ourselves and our camels, and we willingly agreed. They brought us milk at sunset and we drank till we could drink no more. As each of us handed back the bowl from which he had drunk, he said, 'God bless her!', a blessing on the camel who had given the milk. Bakhit and Umbarak turned up next morning, saying that they had expected to find us here. Bakhit was anxious to accompany us to Ibri, where he wished to buy rice and coffee with the money we had given him for the camel. He was afraid to go alone because of the enmity between the Rashid and the Duru.

All the tribes between the Hadhramaut and Oman

belong to one or other of two rival factions, known today as Ghafari and Hanawi. The names themselves date back only as far as a civil war in Oman at the beginning of the eighteenth century, but the division between the tribes which these names denote is very ancient and probably originated in the difference between tribes of Adnan and Qahtan origin. The Duru were Ghafaris, while the Rashid, who were descended from Qahtan, were Hanawis. To travel safely among the Duru we needed a *rabia* or companion, who could frank us through their territory. He could be either from the Duru or from some other tribe entitled by tribal custom to give his travelling companions protection among the Duru while they were in his company. A *rabia* took an oath: 'You are my companions and your safety, both of your blood and of your possessions, is in my face.' Members of the same party were responsible for each other's safety, and were expected to fight if necessary in each other's defence, even against their own tribes or families. If one of the party was killed, all the party were involved in the ensuing blood-feud. No tribe would be likely to attack a party which was accompanied by a tribesman from a powerful tribe to which they were allied, but a *rabia* could belong to a small and insignificant tribe and still give protection. The question of how and where each tribe could give protection was complicated. It often amused my companions to argue hypothetical cases as we rode along, and their arguments sometimes became so involved that I was reminded of lawyers disputing. Our present difficulty was that we should have to penetrate into the

Duru territory without a *rabia* and hope to find one when we arrived there. At present the Rashid and the Duru were not at war, but there was no love lost between them.

Three days later we camped on the eastern edge of the Sands among some scattered thorn-bushes, and the following day we rode for seven hours across a flat plain, whose gravel surface was overspread with fragments of limestone. Ahead of us a yellow haze hung like a dirty curtain across the horizon. We camped in the evening in a sandy watercourse, among some *ghaf* trees. There was a large package of dates in the fork of one of these, left there by its owner in perfect confidence that no one would touch it. At sunset we saw some goats in the distance; but no one came near us. During the night a wolf howled round our camp; it was one of the eeriest sounds I have ever heard.

At dawn I saw a great mountain to the east and Hamad told me that it was Jabal Kaur near Ibri. Later the haze thickened again and hid it from our sight. As we approached the Wadi al Ain, Hamad suggested that he and al Auf had better ride on ahead, in case there was anyone on the well, so that they could give them warning of our approach; otherwise they would certainly shoot at us. They trotted off towards the belt of trees which stretched across our front. A little later, when we arrived near the well, we saw a group of Arabs arguing with Hamad; al Auf came to us and told us to stop where we were as there was trouble. Hurriedly he explained that when they had reached the well they spoke to two Duru who were watering camels, and that these men had been friendly, but that some other Duru, with camels loaded with dates from Ibri, had arrived shortly afterwards and they had declared that no Rashid might use their well. Al Auf then went back to the group round the well, while we waited anxiously to see what was going to happen. Half an hour later he and Hamad came over to us with a young man who greeted us and then told us to unload our camels and make ourselves comfortable; he said that when he had finished watering he would take us to his encampment. The caravan from Ibri watered their animals. One of them unexpectedly gave Hamad a small package of dates; they were very large and very sweet, but I was sick of dates and never wanted to see another. They moved off up the wadi and we then went over to the well, which had clean water at a depth of twenty feet.

In the afternoon the young herdsman, whose name was Ali, led us to his encampment two miles away. Here the Wadi al Ain, the largest of the three great wadis which run down from the Oman mountains into the desert to the west, consisted not of a single dry river-bed, but of several smaller watercourses separated by banks of gravel and drifts of sand. The trees and shrubs that grew here were parched with drought but, even so, they made a pleasant change after the bare gravel plain which we had just crossed.

There were no tents or huts at Ali's encampment. He and his family were living under two large acacias on which they hung their household utensils. They had evidently been here for a long time, since the two brushwood pens in which they put their goats at night were thickly carpeted with droppings. There were two women, both of them veiled, a half-witted boy of four-teen, and three small children. We unsaddled a short distance away from this encampment, in a grove of *ghaf* trees which had been lopped and mutilated to provide grazing for the goats and camels. Ali slaugh-tered a goat for us, and in the evening brought over a good meal of meat, bread, and dates. He was accom-panied by a slave who was spending the night here. Ali agreed to take some of my party to Ibri, although the slave disconcerted us by saying that there had been trouble there a few days earlier between the townsfolk and a party of Rashid. Ali asked me if I was going to Ibri, but I said that I had been suffering from fever and would remain here to rest. Al Auf had told him already that I was from Syria, that I had recently been at Riyadh, and that I was now on my way to Salala. We agreed that bin Kabina and Musallim should remain with me while the others went to Ibri. Ali promised that when he returned from Ibri he would come with us to the Wadi al Amairi, where he could find us another *rabia* to take us through the rest of the Duru country.

The party going to Ibri left in the morning; Ali said that they would be back in five days' time. In the afternoon his father, who was called Staiyun, arrived with a nephew called Muhammad. Staiyun was a kindly, simple old man with a wrinkled face and humorous eyes. He was not likely to ask disconcerting questions, but I was not so sure about Muhammad, who was well dressed, in a clean white shirt, with an expensive woollen head-cloth, and a silver-hilted dagger. He had recently been in Muscat and was obviously a great deal more sophisticated than his uncle. However, he seemed friendly. Staiyun said that it would be better if Muhammad went with us to the Wadi al Amairi instead of his son, but I would rather have had the credulous Ali. It was not going to be easy to live at close quarters with Muhammad for several days and maintain my disguise, since he would soon notice that I did not pray. I was relieved when he said he was going to his own encampment. He promised to come back as soon as Staiyun sent for him. Staiyun confirmed that some Rashid had had trouble at Ibri, but said that they had paid compensation and that all was now well.

They were pleasant, lazy days. Staiyun fed us on bread, dates, and milk and spent most of his time with us. The more I saw of the old man the more I liked him. I asked him about Umm al Samim, and he told me that the three wadis, al Ain, al Aswad, and al Amairi, ended in these quicksands. As far as I could make out they were about fifty miles to the west of us. He confirmed the stories I had already heard that raiding parties had been swallowed up in them, and said that he himself had seen a flock of goats disappear when the ground had suddenly broken up around them; after struggling for a while they had sunk beneath the surface. I determined that I would come back and visit Umm al Samim and that I would try to penetrate into the mountains which were ruled by the Imam. It was interesting to collect from old Staiyun the information I should require to enable me to do this journey: about the tribes and their alliances, the different sheikhs and their rivalries, the Imam's government and where and how it worked, and about wells and the distances that lay between them. But for the present I should be satisfied if I arrived at Bai without mishap and without delay; already I was worried, for five days and then six had passed and still there was no news of my companions.

Staiyun was anxious about his son as a result of the recent trouble in Ibri, and he urged me to go there. He said that if they were in difficulties I could intervene with Muhammad al Riqaishi, the Governor, or even go and see the Imam in Nazwa on their behalf. On the seventh day I decided that I must go in the morning with Staiyun to Ibri. There I should stand revealed as a Christian, and from what I had heard of the Riqaishi and the Imam this would not be pleasant; nor would my intervention help my companions if they were in trouble, but there was nothing else for me to do. It was a great relief when they arrived at sunset. All was well. They pretended that the way was farther than they had expected, but I knew that they had dallied in Ibri enjoying themselves, and I did not blame them.

Next day Hamad and Bakhit returned to their homes, and after Staiyun had fetched Muhammad the rest of us camped on the far side of the wadi. It took us eight hours to reach the Wadi al Aswad and two more long days to reach the Amairi. It was difficult to get the observations which I required for my mapping, and impossible to take photographs while Muhammad was with us. He inquired from the others why I did not pray, and they said that Syrians were evidently lax about their religion.

The Amairi was another large wadi with many trees and bushes. Muhammad took us to the encampment of a man called Rai, who belonged to the small tribe of the Afar, and arranged with him that he should take us to the Wahiba country. The Wahiba are Hanawis and are enemies of the Duru, and none of the Duru could escort us into their country. But the Afar are accepted as *rabia* by both the Duru and the Wahiba. Muhammad went back next day, but we remained for four days, since we had a long way still ahead of us and Rai said that there would be little grazing for the camels once we left the Amairi. Here there had been recent rain and the trees were in leaf. There were many Duru in the wadi, with herds of camels, flocks of sheep and goats, and numerous donkeys. That night I told Rai who I was, since Musallim said that there was no necessity to keep my identity a secret from him. He looked at me and said, 'You would not have got here if the Duru had known who you were', and he warned me to tell no one else. From our camp I could see the long range of Jabal al Akhadar, the Green Mountain, which lies behind Muscat. It rises to ten thousand feet and was still unexplored. I could see other and nearer mountains, none of which were marked on my map. What was shown was guesswork. The Wadi al Ain, for instance, was marked as flowing into the sea near Abu Dhabi. I was more than ever determined to come back and explore this country properly.

I suggested that we should slaughter the *hazmia*, as her soles were wearing thin and she was beginning to go lame, but the others said that there was too many people here and we should have to give all her meat away.

We set off once more. Each interminable, empty day ended at sunset and started again at dawn. The others ate dates before we started, but I could no longer face their sticky sweetness, and I fasted till the evening meal. Hour after hour my camel shuffled forward, moving, it seemed, always up a slight incline towards an indeterminable horizon, and nowhere in all that glaring emptiness of gravel plain and colourless sky was there anything upon which my eyes could focus. I would notice some dots, think that perhaps they were far-off camels, only to realize a few strides farther on that they were stones immediately beneath our feet. I marvelled how Rai kept his direction, especially when the sun was overhead. I knew that camels will never walk straight; my own animal edged off the whole time to the right towards her homeland and I had to tap her back with my stick, a constant source of irritation. Rai and the others talked continuously and seemingly paid no attention to where they were going, and yet when at intervals I checked our course with my compass it never varied more than a few degrees. We reached the well at Haushi near the southern coast six days after leaving the Amairi. For the past two days it had been grievous to watch the limping agony of the *hazmia*. There was nothing here for the camels to eat but the shoots of leafless thornbushes growing in occasional watercourses. The *hazmia* could not even feed. She was accustomed to the grazing of the Sands, and her tender gums could not chew this woody fare. She was becoming thin. Al Auf eyed her and said, 'When we do kill her she won't be worth eating.' We murdered her the evening we got to Haushi. We cut the meat into strips and hung it on bushes to dry, and put the marrow bones into the sac of her stomach, which we tied up with a strip of her skin and buried in the sands, lighting a fire on top of it. Next day when we uncovered it there was a blood-streaked mess floating among the empty bones, which Mabkhaut poured into an empty goatskin. Bedu yearn hungrily for fats, but I dreamt of fruit, of bunches of grapes, and whiteheart cherries. We had hidden ourselves away among sand-dunes but two Wahiba found us there. They were, however, delightful old men, courteous and welcoming, who had not come looking for meat but seeking news and entertainment. They fetched us milk and then spent the night with us. We fed at sunset, eating till we could eat no more. The meat smelt rank and was very tough, the soup was greasy and of a curious flavour, but it was a wonderful meal after all these hungry weeks. Replete at last, I lay on the sand while the old men mumbled reminiscences through toothless gums and the nearby camels belched and chewed the cud.

We spent the next day there drying the meat, and then set off westwards for Bai.

Once more we rode across an empty land, but now it was not only empty, it was dead. Shallow depressions in the limestone floor held sloughs of glutinous black mud, crusted with scabs of salt and sand, like putrescent patches on a carcass rotting in the sun. We rode for seven and eight and nine hours a day, without a stop, and it was dreary work. Conversation died with the passing hours and boredom mounted within me like a dull ache of pain. We muffled our faces against the parching wind, screwed up our eyes against the glare which stabbed into our heads. The flies we had brought with us from our butchers' work at Haushi clustered black upon our backs and heads. If I made a sudden movement they were thick about my face in a noisy questing cloud. I rode along, my body swaying backwards and forwards, backwards and forwards, to the camel's stride, a ceaseless strain upon my back which from long practice I no longer felt. I watched the sun's slow progress and longed for evening. As the sun sank into the haze it became an orange disc without heat or brilliance. I looked at it through my field-glasses and saw the sun-spots like black holes in its surface. It disappeared while still a span above the horizon, vanishing in a yellow sky that was without a cloud.

We reached Bai five days after leaving Haushi. Seeing camels in the distance, Mabkhaut said, 'That is bin Turkia's camel and there is bin Anauf's.' We approached a ridge and suddenly a small figure showed up upon it. It was bin Anauf. 'They come! They come!' he screamed, and raced down the slope. Old Tamtaim appeared, hobbling towards us. I slid stiffly from my camel and greeted them. The old man flung his arms about me, with tears running down his face, too moved to be coherent. Bitter had been his wrath when the

Bait Kathir returned from Ramlat al Ghafia. He said they had brought black shame upon his tribe by deserting me. We led our camels over to their camping place and there exchanged the formal greetings and 'the news'. It was 31 January. I had parted from them at Mughshin on 24 November. It seemed like two years.

Only Tamtaim, bin Turkia, and his son were here. The others were near the coast, where there was better grazing. Bin Turkia said he would take the news to them next day. We slept little that night. We talked and talked, and brewed coffee and yet more coffee, while we told them of our doings. They were Bedu, and no mere outline would suffice either them or my companions; what they wanted was a detailed account of all that we had seen and done, the people we had spoken to, what they had said, what we had said to them, what we had eaten and when and where. My companions seemed to have forgotten nothing, however trivial. It was long past midnight when I lay down to sleep and they were still talking. Next day the others arrived and with them were many Harasis who had come to see the Christian. Some women also turned up. All of them were masked with visor-like pieces of stiff black cloth, and one of them was dressed in white, which was unusual. There was much coming and going and much talk; only Sultan sat apart and brooded. My anxieties and difficulties were now over, but we still had far to go before we reached Salala.

We rode across the flatness of the Jaddat al Harasis, long marches of eight and even ten hours a day. We were like a small army, for many Harasis and Mahra

travelled with us, going to Salala to visit the Sultan of
Muscat, who had recently arrived there. I was as glad
now to be back in this friendly crowd as I had been to
escape from it at Mughshin. I delighted in the surging
rhythm of this mass of camels, the slapping shuffle of
their feet, the shouted talk, and the songs which stirred
the blood of men and beasts so that they drove forward
with quickened pace. And there was life here. Gazelle
grazed among the flat-topped acacia bushes, and once
we saw a distant herd of oryx looking very white against
the dark gravel of the plain. There were lizards, about
eighteen inches in length, which scuttled across the
ground. They had disc-shaped tails, and in consequence the Arabs called them 'The Father of the
Dollar'. I asked if they ate them, but they declared that
they were unlawful; I knew that they would eat other
lizards which resembled them except for their tails.
But, anyway, there was no need now for us to eat
lizard-meat. Every day we fed on gazelles, and twice
Musallim shot an oryx.

We watered at Khaur Wir: I wondered how much
more foul water could taste and still be considered
drinkable. We watered again six days later at Yisbub,
where the water was fresh and maidenhair fern grew
in the damp rock above the pool. We went on again
and reached Andhur, where I had been the previous
year, and camped near the palm grove. Then we
climbed up on to the Qarra mountains and looked
upon the sea. It was nineteen days since we had left
Bai. We descended the mountain in the afternoon
and camped under great fig-trees beside the pools of

Darbat. There were mallard and pintail and widgeon and coots on these pools, and that night Musallim shot a striped hyena. It was one of three which ran chuckling round our camp in the moonlight.

We had sent word into Salala, and next morning the Wali rode out to meet us accompanied by a crowd of townsfolk and Bedu. There were many Rashid with him, some of them old friends, others I had not yet met, among these bin Kalut who had accompanied Bertram Thomas. With him were the Rashid we had left at Mughshin, who told us that Mahsin had recovered and was in Salala.

The Wali feasted us in a tent beside the sea, and in the afternoon we went to the RAF camp. My companions insisted on a triumphal entry, so we rode into the camp firing off our rifles, while ahead of us some Bait Kathir danced and sang, brandishing their daggers.

[. . .]

The Second Crossing of the Empty Quarter

It was a bleak morning with a cold wind blowing from the north-east. The sun rose in a dusty sky but gave no warmth. Bin Kabina set out dates and fragments of bread, left over from the previous night, before calling to us to come and eat. I refused, having no desire for food, and remained where I was, crouching behind a rock, trying to find shelter from the cutting wind and eddies of driven sand. I had slept little the night before, trying to assess the dangers and difficulties which lay ahead. Later, in grey borderlands of sleep, I had struggled knee-deep in shifting sand with nightmares of disaster. Now, in the cold dawn, I questioned my right to take these men who trusted me to what the Saar vowed was certain death. They were already moving about their tasks preparatory to setting off, and only an order from me would stop them. But I was drifting forward, slack-willed, upon a movement which I had started, half-hoping that Salih and Sadr would fail to come and that then we could not start.

Some Saar were already at the well, which would soon be surrounded by Arabs impatient to water their animals. We drove ours down there and filled the troughs, but they would only sniff at the ice-cold water instead of drinking, and drink they must if they were to survive for sixteen waterless days, struggling heavily-

loaded through the sands. Bin Kabina and I went back
to sort the loads, while the others couched each roaring
camel in turn, and, after tying her knees to prevent her
from getting up, battled to hold her weaving neck, so
that they could pour down her throat the water she did
not want. Bin Kabina set aside the rice and the extra
flour to give to Ali. We were taking with us two hundred pounds of flour, which was as much as we could
carry, a forty-pound package of dates, ten pounds of
dried shark-meat, and butter, sugar, tea, coffee, salt,
dried onions, and some spices. There were also two
thousand Maria Theresa dollars, which weighed very
heavily, three hundred rounds of spare ammunition,
my small box of medicines, and about fifty gallons of
water in fourteen small skins. I knew already that several
of these skins sweated badly, but had not been able to
get others from the Saar. Even so, I reckoned that if we
rationed ourselves to a quart each for every day and to a
quart for cooking and coffee, we should be all right, even
if we lost half our water from evaporation and leakage.
This water was sweet, very different from the filthy stuff
we had carried with us the year before. While we were
busy dividing our stores into loads of suitable weight,
Salih and Sadr arrived and I was glad to see that both
their camels were powerful animals in good condition.
We had decided the night before that we would load
the spare camels heavily, at the risk of foundering them
before we reached the Hassi, so as to save our mounts.
I hoped that the two Saar would be able to slip away
unobserved from that well, even if the rest of us were
detained, and it was therefore important that their

camels should be spared as much as possible. They must carry only the lightest loads, if they carried anything at all. I gave them the rifles which I had promised, and fifty rounds of ammunition each. Their friends who had come with them examined these weapons critically, but could find nothing wrong. I had already presented Muhammad and Amair each with a rifle and a hundred rounds of ammunition. Bin Ghabaisha had the rifle I had given him in Saiwun, bin Kabina the one I had given him the year before, and I had my sporting .303, so we were a well-armed party.

The others returned from the well and we loaded the camels. The sun was warmer now and I felt more cheerful, reassured by the good spirits of my companions, who laughed and joked as they worked. Before leaving, we climbed the rocky hill near the well, and Sadr's uncle, a scrawny old man in a loin-cloth, showed us once more the direction to follow, pointing with both his arms. With his wild hair, gaunt face, and outstretched arms he looked, I thought, like a prophet predicting doom. I was almost surprised when he said in an ordinary voice that we could not go wrong, as we should have the Aradh escarpment on our left when we reached the Jilida. Standing behind him I took a bearing with my compass. As we climbed down the hill Ali told me that there had been another fight between the Yam and the Karab near al Abr two days before, and that the bin Maaruf had now decided to abandon Manwakh and to move tomorrow to the Makhia. He said that this was why there were already so many Arabs filling their skins at the well.

We were leaving only just in time. The camels lurched to their feet as we took hold of the head-ropes, and, after each of the Rashid had tied a spare camel behind his own, we moved off on foot. The Saar on the well stopped work to watch us go and I wondered what they were saying. Ali came with us a short distance, and then, after embracing each of us in turn, went back. We had started on our journey, and holding out our hands we said together, 'I commit myself to God.'

Two hours later Sadr pointed to the tracks of five camels that had been ridden ahead of us the day before. At first we wondered if they were Yam, but after some discussion Sadr and Salih were convinced that they were Karab and therefore friendly Muhammad asked me to judge which was the best camel. I pointed at random to a set of tracks and they all laughed and said I had picked out the one which was indubitably the worst. They then started to argue which really was the best. Although they had not seen these camels they could visualize them perfectly. Amair, bin Ghabaisha, and Sadr favoured one camel, Muhammad, bin Kabina, and Salih another. I knew nothing about Sadr and Salih's qualifications, but felt sure that Amair and bin Ghabaisha were right since they were better judges of a camel than Muhammad or bin Kabina. Not all Bedu can guide or track, and Muhammad was surprisingly bad at both. He was widely respected as the son of bin Kalut and was inclined to be self-important in consequence, but really he was the least efficient of my Rashid companions. Bin Ghabaisha was probably the most competent, and the others tended to rely on his judgement, as I did myself. He was certainly the best rider and the best shot, and always graceful in everything he did. He had a quick smile and a gentle manner, but I already suspected that he could be both reckless and ruthless, and I was not surprised when within two years he had become one of the most daring outlaws on the Trucial Coast with a half a dozen blood-feuds on his hands. Amair was equally ruthless, but he had none of bin Ghabaisha's charm. He had a thin mouth, hard unsmiling eyes, and a calculating spirit without warmth. I did not like him, but knew that he was competent and reliable. Travelling alone among these Bedu I was completely at their mercy. They could at any time have murdered me, dumped my body in a sand-drift, and gone off with my possessions. Yet so absolute was my faith in them that the thought that they might betray me never crossed my mind.

We travelled through low limestone hills until nearly sunset, and camped in a cleft on their northern side. The Rashid did not trust the Saar whom we had left at Manwakh, so Amair went back along our tracks to keep watch until it was dark, while bin Ghabaisha lay hidden on the cliff above us watching the plain to the north, which was a highway for raiders going east or west. We started again at dawn, after an uneasy watchful night, and soon after sunrise came upon a broad, beaten track, where Murzuk and the Abida had passed two days before.

Bin Kabina and Amair stayed behind to try to identify some of the looted stock by reading the confusion in the sand. We had gone on a couple of miles when they caught up with us, laughing as they chased each other across the plain. They appeared to be in the best of spirits, and I was surprised when bin Kabina told me that he had recognized the tracks of two of his six camels among the spoil. He had left these two animals with his uncle on the steppes. Luckily, Qamaiqam, the splendid camel on which he had crossed the Empty Quarter the year before, and the other three were with his brother at Habarut. He told us which animals they had been able to identify, but said that there had been so many animals that it was only possible to pick out a few that had travelled on the outskirts of the herd. As I listened I thought once again how precarious was the existence of the Bedu. Their way of life naturally made them fatalists; so much was beyond their control. It was impossible for them to provide for a morrow when everything depended on a chance fall of rain or when raiders, sickness, or any one of a hundred chance happenings might at any time leave them destitute, or end their lives. They did what they could, and no people were more self-reliant, but if things went wrong they accepted their fate without bitterness, and with dignity as the will of God.

We rode across gravel steppes which merged imperceptibly into the sands of the Uruq al Zaza. By midday the north-east wind was blowing in tearing gusts, bitter cold but welcome, as it would wipe out our tracks and secure us from pursuit. We pressed on until night, hoping in vain to find grazing, and then groped about in the dark feeling for firewood. Here it was dangerous to light a fire after dark, but we were too cold and hungry to be cautious. We found a small hollow, lit a fire, and sat gratefully round the flames. At dawn we ate some dates, drank a few drops of coffee, and started off as the sun rose.

It was another cold grey day, but there was no wind. We went on foot for the first hour or two, and then each of us, as he felt inclined, pulled down his camel's head, put a foot on her neck, and was lifted up to within easy reach of the saddle. Muhammad was usually the first to mount and I the last, for the longer I walked the shorter time I should have to ride. The others varied their positions, riding astride or kneeling in the saddle, but I could only ride astride, and as the hours crawled by the saddle edge bit deeper into my thighs.

For the next two days we crossed hard, flat, drab-coloured sands, without grazing, and, consequently, had no reason to stop until evening. On the second day, just after we had unloaded, we saw a bull oryx walking straight towards us. To him we were in the eye of the setting sun and he probably mistook us for others of his kind. As only about three Englishmen have shot an Arabian oryx, I whispered to bin Ghabaisha to let me shoot, while the oryx came steadily on. Now he was only a quarter of a mile away, now three hundred yards, and still he came on. The size of a small donkey – I could see his long straight horns, two feet or more in length, his pure white body, and the dark markings on his legs and face. He stopped suspiciously less than two hundred yards away. Bin Kabina whispered to me to shoot. Slowly I pressed the trigger. The oryx spun

round and galloped off. Muhammad muttered disgustedly, 'A clean miss,' and bin Kabina said loudly, 'If you
had let bin Ghabaisha shoot we should have had meat
for supper'; all I could say was 'Damn and blast!'

I little realized at the time that by missing the oryx
I probably saved our lives. A year later bin al Kamam
joined us on the Trucial Coast. He told us that he had
been at Main in the Jauf, when news arrived that
the Christian and some Rashid were at Manwakh,
preparing to cross the sands. The Governor of the Jauf,
Saif al Islam al Hussain, one of the Imam Yahya's sons,
sent off two parties of Dahm to kill us. The larger party
of twenty occupied some wells on the desert's edge,
which they thought we might visit, while the other
party of fifteen went into the Sands to pick up our
tracks. Bin al Kamam said that he and his companion
had been imprisoned to prevent them from escaping
and giving us warning. He had been certain that the
Dahm would intercept and kill us, and when eventually
he saw them riding back across the plain towards the
town he was waiting to hear that we were dead. Suddenly he realized that they were riding in silence,
instead of singing their war-songs, and that they must
have failed to find us. The smaller party reported that
they had picked up our tracks, which were two days
old; they had followed us for two days, but as we were
travelling very fast they had been afraid that they would
run out of water before they could overtake us. They
said that at our camping places they had seen marks in
the sand where we had put down our bags of gold. If
I had shot the oryx we should have delayed for a day

to dry its meat, and the Dahm would probably have caught up with us. We thought at the time that we were far enough into the Empty Quarter to be safe, and we were not keeping a good look-out. If our pursuers had been from the Yam they would certainly have overtaken us, but the Dahm are afraid of the Sands.

For the next three days we rode across sands where there were only occasional *abal* bushes and a few dry tufts of *ailqi* or *qassis*, the remains of vegetation which had grown after rain four years before. We were now in the Qaimiyat, where parallel dune chains ran from north-east to south-west. These dunes were only about a hundred and fifty feet high, but their steep inclines faced towards us, and the successive floundering ascents exhausted our camels, as they had eaten practically nothing for six days. When we left Manwakh they were very fat, and this gave them reserves on which to draw, but their very fatness distressed them in this heavy sand. They were fresh from pasturage and their backs were soft and unaccustomed to the saddle. Now they were heavily-loaded and doing very long marches. We knew that under such conditions they were certain to develop saddle swellings, which would turn all too easily into ulcers. We would gladly have rested them for a day if we could have found grazing and if our water supply had allowed it. The sheepskins, which I had bought in ignorance, sweated very badly, but we had already finished the water that was in them. Even the goatskins had not been long enough in use to become watertight and we were making constant but ineffectual efforts to check the alarming drip. We passed fresh tracks of oryx and of *rim*, the large white gazelle which is found in the Sands, and knew that if we followed these tracks they would lead us to fresh grazing, but we could not afford to lengthen our journey.

In the afternoon of the sixth day the dune chains turned into gentle downs, but we had already climbed over sixteen of them that day and on one of them a baggage camel collapsed, only moving again when we unloaded her. Bin Kabina's camel went lame in the shoulder, and all the others showed signs of exhaustion. I knew that it would be another ten days before we reached the Hassi and I began to wonder if we should get there.

Next morning we came on the fresh tracks of a pelican which had walked in a straight line across the sand. I tried to remember what it said in the Bible about a pelican in the wilderness. Amair told me that five years earlier he had seen several very large white birds near Mughshin, and that they had left tracks like these. While he was describing these birds we topped a rise and saw that the rolling sands ahead of us were green with *qassis*, growing in tasselled tufts a foot high. We unloaded and turned our camels loose. I knew that this grazing was going to make all the difference to our chance of reaching the Hassi, since it would not only satisfy the camels' hunger but would also alleviate their thirst.

We camped on a floor of hard sand in the shelter of a small dune. Two twisted *abal* bushes, one of them with a broken branch drooping to the ground, three clumps of *qassis*, beside which I had placed my saddle-bags, a pile of camel-droppings, and a low bank of sand, marked with a tracery of lizards' tracks, combined with our scattered possessions to become our home. There were similar places all around us, but, because bin Ghabaisha happened to call out 'Stop over there and we had gone where he had directed, this particular spot acquired a temporary significance. This camping place was memorable because of the grazing, but I always thought each one distinctive at the time. The curious shape of some sticks beside the fire, a sprinkle of white on golden sand where bin Kabina had spilt flour, a rope lying where a camel had jerked it as she rose, such trifles seemed to distinguish each camp from others, but in fact the differences were too insignificant and the memory of them soon blurred. All but a few tended to become just one of a thousand others.

Bin Kabina and bin Ghabaisha were preparing food, and they called out to us, where we lay idly in the sun, that they were going to make porridge flavoured with sugar and butter. Porridge was wasteful of water, but now, contentedly watching the camels ripping succulent mouthfuls from the rich feeding around them, we cheerfully condoned the extravagance. After the meal, bin Ghabaisha and Sadr went off to hunt, but came back empty-handed at sunset, saying they had seen a herd of twenty oryx and many *rim*, but could not get near them. We decided to leave the camels out to graze during the night, feeling that here we were safe from attack. In the morning 'the Red One', the best of our baggage camels, had strayed and it took Amair two hours to find her and bring her back. No camel will ever remain contentedly in one place, however good the grazing, but, even though hobbled, will wander farther afield looking for something better. 'The Red One' was particularly bad at straying, and the others usually followed along behind her. Bin Kabina's camel and Amair's had become inseparable, while mine showed a preference for the *mirri*, an ugly grey, which we had bought in the Raidat because she was in milk. At first she refused to give us any, although her calf had already been weaned, but Amai sewed up her anus, saying he would not undo it until she let down her milk. After that she gave us about a quart a day.

These Bedu allow a camel to suckle her calf without interference for about six weeks; they then cover her udder with a bag, only allowing the calf to drink before they milk her in the morning and evening. They wean it after nine months. A camel will remain in milk for as long as four years provided she is not served by a bull. She may have as many as a dozen calves and has a working-life of about twenty years. These Arabs keep a piece of skin from a calf which has been slaughtered or has died before it was weaned, and allow the camel to smell it before they milk her; otherwise she would not let down her milk.

It was a crisp morning with a gentle breeze. A few white cumulus clouds deepened the blueness of a sky no longer tinged with yellow. Muhammad looked critically at the camels as Amair and bin Ghabaisha drove them towards us, and remarked, 'They look better now. God willing they will be able to reach the

Hassi. Anyway, we may find more grazing. It looks as if there is a lot in the Sands this year, but it is very scattered.' It only took us ten minutes to load, and as we moved off I thought how pleasant it was to be free from the burden of possessions.

We walked across the red downs, and half an hour later came to the end of the grazing. Sadr told me that we had been camped on its eastern edge and that it only extended for four or five miles to the west. We could easily have missed it. A little later, finding some broken ostrich eggs, bin Kabina and Amair argued whether ostriches were lawful food, a purely academic point since ostriches had been extinct in southern Arabia for more than fifty years, although a few survived until recently in the Wadi Sirham in northern Arabia. When I was in Syria a Bedu told me that the Rualla had shot one there just before the war; it may well have been the last of them. My companions stopped to show me what their tracks looked like, saying that their grandfathers had known these birds. I had seen plenty of the tracks of the African ostrich, a larger bird than the Arabian, in the Sudan, and the copies which Amair made in the sand were correct. It is sad to think that the Arabian oryx and *rim* are also doomed as soon as cars penetrate into the southern desert. Unfortunately oryx prefer the hard, flat sands and gravel plains to the heavy dunes. Since they differ from the four species to be found in Africa, it means that yet another kind of animal will soon be extinct. In Saudi Arabia during the last few years even gazelle have become rare. Hunting-parties scour the plains in cars, returning with lorry-loads of gazelle which they have run down and butchered.

Every mile or so I checked our course with my compass; it was difficult to hold everything – the compass, notebook, pencil, camel-stick, and head-rope, especially when the camel fidgeted. I had dropped my stick for the second time when bin Kabina, who jumped down from his camel to pick it up, said as he handed it back to me, 'Really, Umbarak, this is too much. If I were you I should divorce her as soon as you get back.' The Bedu have a saying that whenever a man drops his stick his wife is being unfaithful.

We went on till evening without finding pasturage. When we camped we could see the dark plain of the Jilida six miles away. Bin Daisan had told me that the Jilida linked up with the plain of Abu Bahr, which in turn merged into the plains running down from the Hasa to Jabrin. He had also told me that when we reached the Jilida we should be half-way to the Hassi, but that the big and difficult sands would still lie ahead of us. He had explained that the Aradh escarpment, which ran south from the Hassi, would then be about fifty miles to the west.

Next day we travelled across the Jilida plain. Its surface was of coarse sand and fine gravel, covered in places with small angular pebbles, highly polished by the wind. They were of many kinds: I recognized pieces of porphyry, granite, rhyolite, jasper, and limestone. There were occasional ridges, some of them twenty feet in height, of the quartz conglomerate that underlies the gravel surface of the plain, but these were easily avoided. We travelled fast until midday, when we came on grazing and stopped for two hours. I wandered off to a distant ridge, glad to be alone for a while, and sat watching formless shadows dapple an umber-coloured plain where nothing else moved. It was very still, with the silence which we have driven from our world. Then bin Kabina shouted to me and I went back. Coffee was ready. Muhammad said, 'We thought you were going after those oryx'; and when I asked, 'Which oryx?' he stared at me in amazement. I looked where he pointed and saw them at once, eighteen white dots on the dark plain. Bin Kabina said, 'If they had been Arabs you would have sat there, without seeing them, until they came and cut your throat.' Bedu are always observant; even when they are engrossed in an argument their dark, restless eyes notice everything, and their minds record it. They never daydream.

We found no more grazing and camped at last on flat empty sands beyond the Jilida. We passed much oryx spoor, and saw twenty-eight of them during the day. In the afternoon bin Ghabaisha and I stalked three which we saw ahead of us. As we were getting near them I heard someone calling. Looking round I saw Salih hastening towards us. I thought, 'They have seen Arabs and don't want me to shoot.' When he came up he said, 'Look out or you will give them your wind.' I whispered furiously, 'I hunted animals before you were born. It is you who will frighten them by making such a beastly noise.' Whereupon he merely added to my exasperation by maintaining that oryx did not mind the sound of voices, an inexplicable belief held by some of the Bedu, which probably explains why so few of them succeed in shooting one. I had to take a long shot. I saw that I had hit the one I had fired at, but they all galloped off. We hurried forward and found bloodstains on the ground. When the camels arrived we followed the oryx, but they were going to the south-east and after a while the others refused to go on, saying that we could not afford to lengthen our march by going in the wrong direction. This was so obviously true that I was forced to agree.

Two days later we reached the Bani Maradh. Looking at the mountainous dunes which stretched across our front, I realized that our real difficulties were only now beginning. Fortunately the prevailing winds were different from those in the sands to the south of the Jilida, and in consequence the easier slopes faced south. Even so they imposed a severe strain on our tired camels; they had had only one full meal in the eleven days since we had left Manwakh. If these southern faces had been steep, as in the Uruq al Shaiba the year before, we should never have got over them. Each dune was three to four hundred feet in height, and the highest peaks were built up round deep crescent-shaped hollows. It took us an hour or more to cross each range. Their northern faces fell away in unbroken walls of sand into successive valleys, two miles or more across, which ran down from the Aradh escarpment, and continued until they disappeared from sight twenty miles or more to the east. So far the sands we had passed on this journey had been dreary and uninteresting. Now for the first time the dunes were a lovely golden-red and, although I was tired, hungry, and thirsty, their shapes gave me great pleasure.

Once across the Bani Maradh we were on the southern edge of the *had* pastures on which the Bedu graze their camels, but ours were too thirsty to eat this plant. At midday we came upon tracks, less than a week old, of Arabs and camels, and from now on two of us scouted continuously ahead. We were uncomfortably aware that our own tracks would show any Arab that we had come from the south. A very strong north wind added to our discomfort by filling our eyes and ears with sand, without, however, hiding our tracks, which remained clearly visible in the valley-bottoms where the ground was covered with a mosaic of highly polished limestone fragments.

About four o'clock we decided to stop, so that we could cook a meal and put out the fire before dark. Salih remained to keep watch behind us, and we turned eastwards along the top of the next dune instead of crossing it. Half an hour later we unloaded in a hollow in the downs where our camels could graze without showing themselves upon a skyline. Sadr and bin Ghabaisha stood guard while Muhammad herded the camels, and the rest of us gathered wood and baked bread. The sky was overcast and I could see that it was raining heavily to the west.

When it grew dark we couched the camels, and waited for Salih to come. He arrived an hour later, to report that no one was following us. We fed; everything was cold from the long wait – the coffee, the bread, and the watery gravy from sharkmeat. It was still blowing strongly, and now it had begun to rain. We dared not light a fire and sat talking in whispers. I had just decided to get into my sleeping-bag when bin Ghabaisha signed to us to be quiet and pointed to the camels. They had stopped chewing, and all of them were staring in one direction. Our rifles were already in our hands, during these days we never put them down, and we slid quietly to the ground, crawling to the edge of the small basin in which we had camped. It was too dark to see any-thing, but the camels still watched something, although now they were looking farther to our right. I lay there motionless, straining to see what they saw. Shadows formed and re-formed but I could be sure of nothing. Bin Kabina lay beside me. I touched him inquiringly but he made a sign that he too could see nothing. The cold rain which had soaked through my shirt ran down my flanks, and pattered on my bare legs. The camels started to chew the cud again and were no longer watching. I thought uneasily, 'They are working round behind us.' Amair and bin Ghabaisha evidently thought the same, for they moved farther round to watch the night behind us. Hours later I crawled to my saddle-bags to fetch a blanket, which I shared with bin Kabina. The rest of the night passed very slowly, and nothing happened.

In the morning bin Ghabaisha found the tracks of a wolf that had circled our camp. Muhammad said disgustedly, 'God! Fancy spending the whole night sitting in the rain staring my eyes out trying to see a wolf!', and bin Ghabaisha answered, 'Better be cold and wet than wake up with a dagger in your ribs.'

Wet, cold, and tired, we started early on a cloudy, sunless morning. Later the sun came through and it was very hot, and my thirst grew worse and worse. We passed more fortnight-old tracks of Arabs and their herds. Ahead of us Sadr and bin Ghabaisha scanned each slope and hollow before they signed to come on. The rest of us dragged the trembling camels up the slopes, and held them back as they ploughed down the far side of each dune in cascades of sand. It was weary work and all the time I felt that we were being watched. The dunes were now about five hundred feet high and at the western end of each valley we could at last see the dark wall of the Aradh. We stopped after nine hours when the camels could go no farther, again cooking a quick meal before sunset, and eating it in the dark after Sadr, who had been watching our tracks, had joined us. For the first time on this journey there was a heavy dew. We slept fitfully, jerking to wakefulness whenever a camel stirred. It was fine and clear when we started again at sunrise. Two hours later one of the baggage camels lay down and refused to move, until, at Amair's suggestion, we poured a little water down her nostrils, which revived her. We reached the Aradh at one o'clock and camped two hours later in a shallow watercourse on the limestone plateau. We were across the Sands.

The valleys when I woke at dawn were filled with eddying mist, above which the silhouettes of the dunes ran eastwards, like fantastic mountains towards the rising sun. The sky glowed softly with the colours of the opal. The world was very still, held in a fragile bowl of silence. Standing at last on this far threshold of the Sands I looked back, almost regretfully, the way we had come.

We reached the Hassi three days later, after travelling northward across a gravel plain scattered with pieces of limestone. The precipitous western edge of the Aradh was on our left. Beneath it were the three shallow wells of Zifr, and thirty miles to the north of them was the deep, brackish well of Qariya, among the ruins of a Sabaean city.

According to Sadr the well mounds of Mankhali, believed by the Bedu to be the wells of the Bani Ad, lay at the southern end of the Aradh; and their lost city of Ad under the sands of Jaihman, a further day's journey to the south. Muhammad was, however, convinced that this city, one of the two mentioned in the Koran as having been destroyed by God for arrogance, was buried in the sands to the north of Habarut. He reminded me of the many clearly defined tracks which converge on these sands, and which the Rashid maintain once led to that city. Sadr pointed beyond the sands of Bani Ramh to some peaks visible far to the west, which were, he said, in the foothills of the Hajaz, and I told them how I had visited that country two years before. When I told them that I had ridden through it on a donkey they scoffed at me and we argued happily as we went along.

On the second day after leaving the Sands we

camped in the stream bed of the Hanu, that runs down to Qariya; and next morning, as we rode along the track to the Hassi, we came unexpectedly on eight mounted Yam, whose rifles were slung under their saddles, while ours were in our hands. We were only a few yards from them. I saw bin Ghabaisha slip his safety-catch forward. There was an old man opposite me, and though his face was muffled in his head-cloth I could see the hatred in his eyes. No one moved or spoke. The silence was heavy between us. At last I said 'Salam alaikum,' and he replied. A boy whispered to him, 'Are they Mishqas?' and he snarled back without taking his eyes off us, 'Don't you know the tribes? Don't you know the foe?' Muhammad said that we came in peace, that we were Rashid from the eastern sands on our way to visit Ibn Saud, adding that our main party was close behind and advising them to be careful when they met them. We then rode on. I wondered uneasily what we should have done with them if we had surprised them in the Sands. Perhaps if we had taken their rifles and their camels we could have let them live. Twenty minutes later we were at the Hassi. It was sixteen days since we had left Manwakh.

Having watered our camels and filled our skins, we learnt from some women that Ibn Saud's guardian on the well had just gone off with his son to look for a strayed camel. Sadr and Salih were anxious to seize this opportunity and slip away before he returned. We loaded their camels, which were still in good condition, with all the food and water that they could carry, and as the women had told us that the Yam had all moved westwards a week ago and that the sands to the south were empty, we hoped that they would be all right. To avoid arousing suspicion we told the women that they were going to fetch one of our camels which had collapsed two days earlier. We whispered our farewells, embraced them, and they left us. They arrived safely at Manwakh, as I later heard from bin al Kamam when I met him on the Trucial Coast.

There was nothing for us now to do but to go to Sulaiyil and hope for the best. Our camels were in need of rest; we had very little food and no guide. Even if we had been able to slip away, a pursuit party would certainly be sent after us. The guardian of the well, a Yam, returned next day and made no attempt to conceal his dislike of us. When he learnt that I was a Christian he refused to drink the coffee we offered him, saying that I was an infidel and that my companions, as Muslims who had sold themselves into the service of an infidel for gold, were even worse. Virtually under arrest, we went with him to Sulaiyil, where we arrived two days later.

The oasis extended for about two miles along the Wadi Dawasir, and the settlement itself consisted of five small villages. On our way to the village where the Amir lived we passed fields of wheat and lucerne, watered from trip-buckets raised from the wells by animals descending ramps. There were palms to the west of the village. The Yam led us down narrow, twisting lanes. Some men called out asking who we were, and he answered scornfully, 'An infidel and his servants.' We stopped at the Amir's house, flat-roofed and made of mud, like all the others.

Rather to my surprise, the Amir, who was a young slave, received us graciously. He showed us to an empty house with a courtyard on the outskirts of the village and, after saying that we should of course feed with him, told us that we must remain at Sulaiyil until he heard from Ibn Saud. He and one of his retainers, a Murra who knew the Rashid, and two young wireless operators were the only friendly people. Everyone else was fanatical and unpleasant. The elders spat on the ground whenever we passed, and the children followed me round chanting derisively, '*Al Nasrani, al Nasrani,*' the name by which these Arabs know a Christian. In the evening we bought lucerne, but only Muhammad's camel would eat it. When after supper we gave the Amir an account of our journey, he said: 'You do not realize how lucky you have been to get here. I should not have thought that you would have had a chance. The sands you came through were filled with Arabs until a week ago, when most of them moved westward across the Aradh to better grazing. If a single Arab had seen you, the hue-and-cry would have been out, for they would have known at once that you are from the south. Didn't you know that Ibn Saud has given permission to his tribes to raid the Mishqas and to kill any of them they meet, in revenge for the recent raids on the Yam and the Dawasir? They are wildly excited here at having permission to raid after years of enforced peace. Many parties have gone off and others are getting ready to go. Any of them would have killed you out of hand if they had met you; nothing could have saved you if they had found that one of you was a Christian. These tribes are the last of the *Akhwan*. Even in this village, where they are under control, you can see how they hate you as an infidel.' He looked at me, shook his head, and said again, 'By God, you were lucky!'

I knew he was right and realized how badly I had misjudged our chances. This realization increased the responsibility I felt towards my companions, who had appreciated the true risks and yet had come with me.

Two days later the Amir came to our room to tell me he had received orders by wireless from Ibn Saud to detain the Englishman and to imprison his companions. He removed our rifles and daggers, told me to remain where I was, leaving the Murra as a guard, and ordered Muhammad and Amair to follow him. He said that bin Kabina and bin Ghabaisha, who were herding the camels, could wait till the evening. When I protested at being separated from my companions, and asked that we should be treated alike, he said he must obey the King's orders, but allowed me to send a telegram to Ibn Saud.

After several efforts I composed a telegram saying that we had been travelling in the Empty Quarter and had come to the Hassi for water. I asked for his forgiveness, adding that if he wished to punish anyone I was solely to blame, since my companions, who had no knowledge of this country, had gone where I wished and that it was I who had guided them.

In the evening, I saw bin Kabina and bin Ghabaisha coming towards the village with the camels. They looked very cheerful, laughing and joking together. The Murra allowed me to meet them and tell them what had happened. Seeing me, some children called out, 'Now the King will cut off the Christian's head and the heads of his companions.' I was so distressed that I could hardly speak. They had trusted me and I wondered unhappily whether they were now going to suffer for it. I felt worse about them than I did about the others, for they were so much younger. They asked a few questions, and then bin Kabina put his hand on my shoulder and said, 'Don't worry, Umbarak; if God wills, all will be well.'

At sunset the Amir did his best to cheer us up with a meal in his house, but it was an unhappy evening. Hours later when I was half asleep the door was thrown open. A large black slave came in swinging a pair of fetters, and ordered me to get up and go with him at once, as the Amir of the Wadi had arrived. I followed through silent streets to the Amir of Sulaiyil's house.

The room was packed with people. An elderly bearded man in a brown gold-embroidered cloak re-turned my formal greeting, bidding me sit opposite him. His clerk, a shifty-looking, self-important slave whom I disliked on sight, was bullying Amair. 'Don't lie,' he shouted after every answer. 'You only know how to lie.' Eventually the Amir asked me where we came from and why. I explained that I had come from the Hadhramaut, that I had been exploring and shooting oryx in the Empty Quarter and, having run out of water, had come to the Hassi. I told him that the Rashid, who were with me, knew neither the country nor where we were going. He asked me how in that case we had found the Hassi, and I said that Philby had marked it on the map, and that the two Saar who had been with us had known where it was, having visited it from Najran. I said they had gone back when we reached this well. I insisted that I alone was to blame for having come here, and accepted all responsibility.

Later, after coffee and tea had been handed round, the Amir of the Wadi said I must go with him to Dam, and that one of my companions could come with me. I asked for bin Kabina. Eventually the two of us climbed into the back of the Amir's truck, the slave who had fetched me from my room got in with us, still holding the fetters. After the Amir, his clerk, and the driver had mounted in front, we drove off to the west. It was very cold, the car lurched and bumped, and bin Kabina was car-sick. He had told me as we waited to get into the car that all four of them had been put in the stocks, when suddenly a messenger arrived and asked which was bin Kabina. I said the Amir had given permission for one of them to accompany me and that I had asked for him. He replied, 'You should have asked for Muhammad. He is the eldest.'

At last we arrived at another village and stopped in front of a large castle. The slave informed us that we were at Dam. We followed the Amir inside, and he gave orders for tea and coffee to be made, and a fire to be lit where we could warm ourselves. He told me that he had seen my telegram to the King, and said, 'Don't worry. I am sure that all will be well.' Then he bade us good night and left the room.

The slave came in again with some quilts for our bedding. He asked if we wanted more coffee and when we refused helped himself and went out. The fire died down and the room grew very dark. The wind banged a loose shutter throughout the night.